MW01480326

A VISTA VOLUNTEE R IN NORTH CAROLINA -1968-1969-

What follows are the scattered thoughts of this 1968 college graduate who, after said graduation, and subsequent rejection by the Military, immediately went to North Carolina TO become and DID become a VISTA VOLUNTEER for one year!

As a Volunteer, he ran a program called: JOBMOBILE. The report written based on the Jobmobile Project, is towards the back of this Book.

(NOTE: The Front-Cover Page contains a photo of myself and the Jobmobile Van).

Full Article and picture

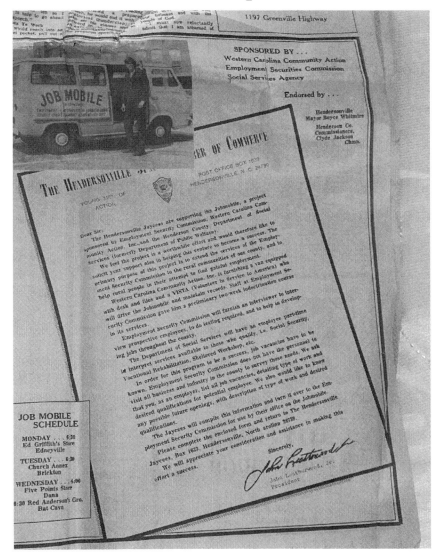

CONTENTS

PART I
OVERVIEW/SUMMARY

PART II
DEPARTURE for NORTH CAROLINA

PART III
TRAINING IN THE BOONIES

PART IV –
JOBMOBILE

PART I

OVERVIEW

and

SUMMARY

I initially flew to Charlotte, North Carolina (We eventually learned the native rural pronunciation was: "NOR KLINA").

We were trained in a university called JOHNSON C SMITH UNIVERSITY. For three weeks we learned the overall purpose of the program and were educated as to what it all meant. Mostly classroom but several times we went into Charlotte to work together on projects AND experience the reality of inner cities.

After those three weeks, those of us who were kept went on out to rural areas. We spent another three weeks out there, again, learning more and more. Those who were still kept on, graduated from the program, and became: VISTA VOLUNTEERS. We all were sent to various sites/towns throughout the State for our final experiences.

I went from the Eastern part of the state then to a place called Henderson County in Western North Carolina, where I ran a startup program called: JOBMOBILE.

In any area we were assigned, we spent a great deal of time traveling around local rural areas experiencing a great number of things.

I departed the state to return to Portland, Oregon in August of 1969.

(NOTE: I use the word "I" a SIGNIFICANT amount, - as this is indeed, sadly, mostly about me)!

(BUT BEFORE WE BEGIN, I WILL DISCUSS MY FINAL COLLEGIATE DAYS - AND OTHER **SIGNIFICANT** MATTERS OF THE TIME SIGNIFICANT MATTERS OCCURING JUST BEFORE GOING OFF TO NORTH CAROLINA.

I attended the University of Portland in Portland, Oregon from 1964 to 1968. It is a small, Catholic College. My Major was American History with a Social Sciences Minor.

During the 1960s University Professors were driven to provide a rigorous education. They were themselves very well educated, some having to take their oral exams in Greek and/or Latin!

We were assigned lots of work, including papers and long-term projects. Little mercy was shown. No matter how hard you worked it never seemed quite enough for the Professors!

I was a day student and had to work nights and weekends for the entire four years to pay for tuition, books etc. (Towards the end, I filled orders at a Montgomery Ward's Warehouse and had to do so on roller skates!) So, I never got a full-time student experience. It was tough but it was well worth the effort as I learned a great deal that

I was able to use throughout my life.

1- MARTIN LUTHER KING

On April 4 of 1968, Martin Luther King was shot and killed. Everyone was more than a bit tense. Rioting and general anger infused the Country.

Montgomery Wards, where I was working, had us lock up the gun cage and then the guards swarmed throughout the building.

There was window breaking and street rioting in Portland, but nothing happened at Wards. A major Avenue (ironically Union) that generally divided the Black/White areas, had considerable damage done to it, especially stores, and the surrounding neighborhoods.

(After the riots, the new stores that came back were often strongly reinforced to allow shopkeepers to protect their properties. It made the neighborhood a little less carefree appearing but still most reopened later in the year).

2- ROBERT FRANCIS KENNEDY!

Then Robert F Kennedy came to the University of Portland a short while after the MLK shooting. It was on a Thursday. He spoke at the University of Portland's main Assembly Hall.

Shortly after entering and seating myself, he began speaking. I slowly realized he was giving the <u>exact same speech</u> he had given on TV earlier in the week!

I figured "what the heck:" Why not leave now and go out front, wait for him and shake his hand when he comes out to get into his Limo and at least have that memory! (Believe his Limo was a 1956 Black Lincoln Convertible).

I then figured his Secret Service would block me, but why not at least try? So, I stood in front of his Limo waiting for him to come out the same doorway he had gone in. After about 20 minutes, out he came.

I stood my ground as throngs of people poured around me. Then here he came, right where I figured/hoped and prayed he might. I shook his hand first and boy was it rough. Then his wife came next and I shook her hand too. Her hand was a little rough but not as bad as his. I was later told it was their sail-boating that roughened them up!

Later that day I was thinking about how easy it was for me to get near his car and stand there waiting for him. No one questioned me or my presence.

About two weeks later (June 5, 1968), a couple I knew, Peter and Candy and I, were planning on going to San Francisco for a few days. We were at

Sears the night before our departure, in the TV section when we saw a bulletin that RFK had just been shot while leaving an event in Los Angeles!

We understood he was being led out through the back of a restaurant where a guy was waiting for him, (Sirhan-Sirhan).

I never ever forgot that sequence of events- how available he was to strangers then and how that easy accessibility might have cost him his life. (And we did take our trip to San Francisco like we planned, but a lot of the spirit was lost).

I did notice they really tightened up security for Politicians after that, despite the fact even **more** got shot and shot at AND several plots were broken up as well.

3. ENLISTING AND BEING DRAFTED

But, back to reality. I realized my DRAFT NOTICE would soon be coming and I would end up going into the Marines (apparent shortage at that moment)!!

My only hope was the fact that in April of 1967 I had had a possible draft deferment in the form of a collapsed lung (Spontaneous Pneumothorax).

BUT any hope of a deferment was dashed by the letter my MD gave me in April of 1968 that said I was actually better off than before the collapsed lung!

So then to avoid the draft, I applied to VISTA (a program the sister of a friend of mine had joined).

But fearing a swift draft call by the military, I also enlisted in the Army. (I did so to avoid having to join the Marines!). Yeah, don't judge me!

Ironically, I got drafted AND was called to report right away. I said my goodbyes to family and friends and reported to the Induction Board. There were numerous protestors (Viet Nam War Era). I stepped over their bodies, gave them Peace Signs, and with other inductees, just quietly went on in.

Once in, we were brought to a large room and stood side by side in rows. After some fumbling around they discussed the process we would be undergoing.

They then jovially announced that the group prior to ours had been sent down to Fort Ord for the Marines. They added that this would have happened to us if the previous group had not been sent!

We all protested loudly and said it did not seem fair. But they explained, with big grins, that that was the Military Way!

I went through most of the induction process, even getting sworn in. I passed all the various phases: Hearing, seeing, even coughing while standing in a large circle.

But then I showed the damning letter from my MD to a couple Military MDs.

I feared the worst, but they looked at it then at me and they gave me a blue card and told me to go to Room 9 on the 3rd floor. I had no clue what was going on, especially since my MD's letter basically gave me up.

A lot of us went into room 9 and just sat there. We were quietly seated for about 10 minutes - not knowing what to expect. It was clear that several of the people waiting appeared to have health-related issue but nothing so obvious as to be a reason to be rejected.

Eventually a military guy came in and asked to see each of our cards. <u>After carefully reviewing and then signing them, he announced we all had been rejected for health/physical/psychological reasons!</u>

Lots of guys were happy about it. I was happy too, but also life confused. I had made no long-term life or career plans outside of the draft. I figured if I survived Viet Nam, I would have had a couple more years to figure things out.

And several people were upset because they had been dropped off by friends from about 200 miles away. They were "kinda screwed" with no money and no way out of Portland.

Some of the guys were also expecting to make a career out of the military. They had made their goodbyes to families and girlfriends before they started the induction process. It was very painful for many.

When I left the building heading for home later that afternoon, there were no longer any protestors. I stepped over no one.

The bus ride home was without incident. I walked from the bus stop to our house thinking all the way what I would say. So many people, me included, were thinking I might not be back, ever.

Everyone who saw me was amazed and asked what happened and how this could be. So many of my friends were drafted, successfully, so it was indeed a good question.

After the tumult died down, I had to start thinking about a future. I had no plans, no future, nothing. My friends had all gotten into something right after College, either a master's Program or some type of job, professional or otherwise.

VISTA ACCEPTANCE

But then, "lo and behold," I got an acceptance letter from VISTA. I rejoiced, sort of! While it was somewhat unexpected, it truly was something.

But I really wanted to join mainly because of my friends who went into VISTA who had described it as such a great and rewarding experience.

My sister was also inspirational as she was currently serving in the Peace Corps and explained how wonderful that was. In numerous letters she explained what she had done and was going through, which all sounded exciting and, most importantly, useful.

PART II

DEPARTURE for NORTH CAROLINA

Over a period of a very few days, I again said goodbye to friends and relatives … this time to go into VISTA. A week or so later, I packed my bags and was driven out to the Portland Airport.

It was a fine sunny morning when I flew out in July of 1968. I first landed at O'Hare in Chicago. We departed and I landed in the late afternoon, on one fine sunny late afternoon in Charlotte, North Carolina.

VISTA Leaders met several of us at the airport then drove us to Johnson

C. Smith University where we met everyone else.

AND WHO WERE WE VISTAS?

We got to the building and were led to a large room with lots of chairs aiming toward the front of the room. We sat and looked around, occasionally speaking to each other.

We consisted of people of all ages, genders, demeaners and interpersonal skills.

Religiously, we soon found out we VOLUNTEERS consisted primarily of Jews, Christians and Catholics. Of course, the few others were agnostics. But Religion was something we all discussed occasionally throughout our VISTA time.

We varied in age from 18 on up with most being under 26. About 50/50 boy/girl.

Educationally, most were recent college as well as some recent high school graduates.

Lots of the women had taken teacher preparation and just put off teaching for the one year.

FIRST PARTNERS/ROOMIES

(Roommates)

After our initial meet and greet, we stayed for a couple hours while they gave us an overview and assigned us partners with whom we would room the next three weeks.

Steve and I were assigned as roomies. He and I hit it off well. He did not have a degree yet but was very bright and not averse to taking risks.

(He noted he was working in the basement of a Hospital in San Francisco at the time. He said they were filming BULLIT then and he ran into Steve McQueen walking toward him in the basement of the facility. He said he just said "hello" and Steve said the same back! Kind of a cool event/memory!)

Steve and I ended up being taken about 8 blocks from the school where we stayed in the home of a genuinely nice Black Woman. She checked up on us nightly! However, she was very unmemorable as I have no specific remembrances of her like I do for so many others. Go figure.

Each day, we walked through a somewhat dangerous part of Charlotte but that was what VISTA wanted us to experience-being in places we had never been to before. What lay ahead for the next three weeks was a great learning opportunity/experience!

ROUTINES and PEOPLE

ROUTINES

We would get up around 7 each day, eat some eggs and cereal (homemade) and walk the eight or so blocks to the school each morning - arriving around 9 am. We would get together as a large (probably 40 of us) group where they trained us in what we would be facing.

We watched several films each day and were lectured by various Program Trainers/Instructors. Some of us took copious notes AND received tons of handouts ... much like college. (There were no tests, thank goodness).

MEMORABLE PEOPLE

One Vista wannabe a group of us met was a guy from California. He had long blond hair, beach tan, Surfer body. He was stunning-by any gender measure.

Soon after that, we met a beautiful/gorgeous/stunning girl from Massachusetts! She was out of our league. They looked like a perfect match for each other. We expected them to meet and turn it into a fairy tale story/ending.

Inevitably, after a couple hours, those two encountered each other. They immediately started circling and staring at each other. A gain, I thought "what a perfect match! They are an ideal couple!" But they soon walked away from each other and introduced themselves to others.

However, we found out, they had known each other from a year earlier. Last time they saw each other was in London where they were to be married. On their wedding day, the Surfer never showed up at the Church...he just left England and her at the altar!

Again, they seemed/looked so ideal for each other, but I was wrong about that. I later realized it would indeed be tough to be around each other for long. The odds of them meeting like that...

Neither stuck around in Charlotte for exceptionally long. The blond surfer left first and the girl a day later... in tears. We, of course, never heard any more.

One older woman was a delight. However, she was picked up by her grandchildren and hustled on out within a couple weeks. She presumably was taken back to their home. They never said anything to us or the VISTA people. She was just rushed on out.

She told us her family originally had promised her she could stay if she wanted. But apparently, they just got too upset. She had and showed a great heart but apparently the family just did not want her there.

There was nothing we nor the VISTA program could say to stop them. We were all disappointed because she had a square and gentle head on her shoulders and taught us a lot. Sad to watch her being taken out against her will. Long live people like her!!

As noted above the rest of us were college grads under 26. We were from all over the country.

VERY SMALL and PETTY MOSTLY GUY TALK

At our group VISTA meetings, we guys sometimes would talk about strictly guy stuff. There were several jokes some guys made about VISTA GIRLS. "They were there to get married, there to forget a boyfriend," and last but not least, "there to actually do and learn."

Presumably, the girls talked about us guys in the same way, but we never knew for sure.

NOTE:

One thing one of the VISTA Instructors told us was that locals would accuse us all of being: "**Pointy headed, briefcase totin', left wing liberal Jews from New York City!**"

I had never heard that phrase before, but it sticks with me today. Pretty hardcore statement, but never **heard** any North Carolinian saying anything like that to my face. However, they might have, unbeknownst to me, have said it. And it was, off and on, in the back of my mind.

TRAINING

We had lots of training. It consisted of lectures and movies, the lectures usually following a movie.

One of the training movies they showed us was of an interview of an older Black Man surrounded by White Men taking place in some kind of office.

They were asking the Black gentleman if he would prefer a Black doctor over a White one, the same with other professions. In each case he responded that he would want only a White one.

When asked why he said because he did not think the Black ones would be as good a White one.

Our instructor asked us why we thought the Black man would say such things. I quickly replied that it was because he had either been paid to do so or was threatened. Others had similar thoughts.

The instructor said "no" that it was because the gentleman believed it! He went on to explain that after generations of being told something, people will begin to believe it!

The instructor used that film to help explain how people could believe such things. We all realized how severe the problems were/and were going to be.

OUR ROLE

One of the NUMEROUS principles of community organizing that VISTA was going to teach us, was to help people find their way out of these beliefs.

It appears this was a lesson Blacks had not learned very well so far. BUT NC was considered the most advanced racially sensitive state in the in the South. We could only imagine what the rest of the South was like.

BUT North Carolina was very progressive in many respects. Basically, I eventually found out that most of the people in power really wanted to transfer the State from exclusionary to inclusive. They wanted it not for economic considerations but basically "It was the right thing to do!"

EXPERIENCES OTHER THAN OFFICIAL TRAINING

Our Instructors' task/goal was to get us involved in parts of the neighborhoods. They wanted us to interact with poor Blacks (primarily) as we were in a predominately Black neighborhood.

One afternoon after class, some of us went to a local theater located in a very Black part of Charlotte. Kind of risky from a White point of view but my roomie Steve said it was a great opportunity.

The movie involved both Black and White slaves in Roman times. One scene was where a Princess had to choose which slave would die for her. She looked at them all and one tall handsome Black guy was there and she said: "If someone has to die for me, it might as well be the most beautiful." Everyone in the theater turned and looked at us and clapped and cheered!

SWORDSMAN

One of our local neighbors across the street from our house was an old,

Black gentleman. He wore shorts and a large silver necklace. He walked around carrying a bright, polished sword. It appeared heavy and it was shiny and silver.

He explained he/we lived in a rough area and he made it clear to the toughs that he was armed and ready to use it. He never had any problems before or from what we could see, during the three weeks we were there. He was tough and erratic acting and spookily old!

PARTY

We also got invited to a party by our Black neighbors' mother. Two Whites with about 30 Blacks. Lots to drink, dancing, having fun, great music. Not a lot of interaction with us however, except by the mother. People seemed kind of embarrassed to say the least.

As the evening went on, things got louder and more fun for us. But eventually there were some disagreements between some of the partiers and things began to melt down. We politely left around 10 but overall had a great time before things got louder.

THE WALK

A week or so later, Steve and I were walking back from our daily class training. It was pretty-dark with few streetlights. We saw several Black guys hanging around the street corner across from us. Steve suggested we go talk to them and so we (me very reluctantly) ran across the street and met up with them. They were kind of dumbfounded we did, so but did talk a few seconds.

The Leader identified himself as Big John. After a few words he said they would like some wine. So, we said we would get some and we went back across the street and bought a bottle of wine and brought it back.

They walked us a few blocks away from the main street and they and their friends opened the bottle of wine and drank it down. After about 20 minutes several of them said they had to get up early, so they were leaving. As we were in a pretty rough area, we asked if anyone would walk us back.

Big John, as well as his "followers" took us down the street. We got a couple blocks down when we realized we had forgotten our textbooks! He walked us back but told us we were on our own after that. We did not run into anyone after that and got back to our place.

We told the Teaching Staff the next day what and who we had encountered. They were amazed. They said they had been trying to make contacts with BIG JOHN for months with no luck. They quizzed us in some detail. But we never ran into him again.

On weekends we VISTAs occasionally met each other for dinner. Cabs were cheap so we could all meet somewhere, and we got to know each other better and better. Some of the boy/girl stuff worked out well, at least in the short term.

OTHER INFO...

We had two CO Vistas who were former Peace Corps Volunteers who were putting their training and field experience to good use. They were telling us about when they were in Peru at a Peace Corps welcoming party. One of the Peruvian Officials commented how Americans could think so little of Black people and asked why they were so mistreated.

One of the former Peace Corps Volunteers explained in detail how Racism and Prejudice had all come about in the US and was being dealt with. The Peruvian Officials did/could not "get it" so the Volunteer tried another tact.

He asked the Officials how Indigenous Peoples were treated in Peru. They started to explain how troubling and bothersome and dishonest they were, when one of them suddenly "GOT IT." They never got any more questions about how racism could still exist in the US.

Another soon to be VISTA was telling us about the MARTIN LUTHER KING "I have a Dream" speech.

He said he was in DC for the event and was there when he made the actual speech. BUT he said when Martin Luther King was talking, he was wandering around looking for a toilet.

He said he missed the most important speech ever, because of his endless trek!

And More. As we were in a City College every day and even though it was summer break, there were a lot of kids taking summer courses. Others who seemingly were just there hanging around.

We met two Black girls playing ping-pong in a room on the ground floor near the gym. They offered to play us and so we took them up.

At first, they seemed to find a couple of us challenging. But then they started being themselves and cleaned ours clocks!

They seemed better than their age and were good. We soon realized they could beat any of us without much effort. Turns out one was the STATE CHAMPION and her friend was a runner up!

We chatted and played at playing with them for about 10 minutes. We were soon convinced that "persistence was futile!" We stopped occasionally to talk about race relations and how things were changing… or not.

They told us they used to not be able to go to a clothing store and try on clothes as they were Black. They explained that one of their friends who was nearly White would enter the store with them.

She would try clothes on, and when she was done, she would, in her Blackest voice, scream that it "weren't no good for her skin!" She and her friends would then run laughing out of the store!

They had several stories like that, but they were now allowed full access.

The final Charlotte Event:

Fingerprinting.

Towards the last days, we were taken to the Charlotte Sheriff's department to be fingerprinted for our FBI records. (Yes, I probably have a file/record… or at least had one at one time).

The office was filled with mostly White male officers with a sprinkling of Blacks. Several non-deputy females were there too.

Interestingly the Deputies, regardless of race, looked remarkably similar. Mostly in great shape, apparently ex-GIs, sharp and alert. Not the typical stereotypes of Southern cops.

Interestingly, on the wall was a photo of a Black guy with a knife blade stuck right into the side of his skull! His eyes were wide open. I could not tell if he was dead as there was no blood and he appeared to be looking straight ahead. Weird photo- probably some kind of warning? We never asked about it.

In the office we were in, a Black and a White deputy were working side by side. They got antsy towards each other while we were there, both offering to "settle this once and for all" if the other cared to. No one intervened that we could see/hear.

They eventually both spun around and sat at their respective desks and said nothing more, though they occasionally glared at one another. It could have been racial, but it might have been personal. We did not know.

We were all taken to another room and were separately brought into an inner office. They asked us some questions and fingerprinted each of us. After about an hour of that process we were led out and were sent on our way back to our group.

PART III

TRAINING IN THE BOONIES

After three weeks of school training at Johnson C. Smith and the finger printing, we were transferred out to the Boonies. My friend Steve was assigned to someone else as was I.

Kent was my new roomie and we stayed together, first for three weeks, then our permanent assignment for several months (until I went into Jobmobile in Eastern North Carolina in January of 1969).

During our first week of field work in the boonies, we got together as a whole unit, probably 30 of us VISTAS, several times at a local Government building. We received more training, got questions answered and we were always quizzed about our desire to continue.

Apparently, they had lots of other Vista groups where many would just suddenly and inexplicably drop out. So far, we were a tight-knit group, except those noted above and a few others who just disappeared.

Sometimes no one quit, other times 1-2 might quit. We never saw "the departed" again and they never saw us either. Do not think any of us were ready to NOT SEE some very nice people. It could be painful.

FIRST PROJECT/TRAINING was:

BRICK MAKING AND BRICK LAYING

Our VISTA Supervisors took a bunch of us to a field next to where a County Jail was being erected. The chief bricklayer there was introduced as our Instructor/Teacher.

The Instructor herded us into a little bus for a ride so we could see what real brick walls looked like. While driving along, he slowed down to show us one house he claims had poorly laid bricks.

He harangued about the bricklaying techniques for several seconds. We of course quietly thought it was a good-looking place. He finally figured we did not understand the "nuance" of brick laying and he resumed driving.

Back at the Jail, we were first shown how to make these kind of sun bricks (did not need to be baked like real bricks). We were taught to make them out of sand and concrete and water. Then we ran them through compacter and then BRICKED them by laying them out in the sun.

He taught us how to hold and place the bricks AFTER we used real mortar to "glue" them together. We got more and more into it and eventually spent a couple days actually laying bricks pretty well. We eventually became "decent" brick makers and layers.

VISTA got this idea from the PEACE CORPS work in South America. Down there they were able to make the bricks, lay them and later roof and door them. And people learned to make them, and the program was a huge self-perpetuating success.

So, they had us learn the proper mix, how to use the device to compress them and lay them out to dry for a few days.

The VISTA Program wanted us to learn the process then for us to teach the locals how to build their own low-cost homes. It was a great idea and we were all anxious to learn all there was to know.

In the meantime, the guy teaching us was also laying "REAL" bricks for a new County Jail. He let us practice laying "REAL" bricks on HIS wall while our home-made bricks were drying/hardening.

(He later revealed that the bricks we laid for the County Jail were not quite done right and that he would remove them each night after we left and redo them all). A real perfectionist to say the least.

He explained he had to have everything done perfectly and we just were not there yet. But after a few days of making and bricking we got a little bit better.

HOWEVER, as we were continuing working on learning the brick laying trade, (about the fifth day) the VISTA Leaders came out and announced that the North Carolina Department of Construction (or some such Agency) chose NOT to approve OUR bricks because they did not meet hurricane or earthquake standards. Apparently, they were too light (lacked tensile strength) and could not take any such stresses.

So, we were summarily dismissed from that project with little to show for our efforts except for some skills AND a brick each that we had made from sand and cement!

I took mine home and I still use it as a paper weight and/or a book end- fifty plus years later!

INTERESTING INTERACTIONS & EXPERIENCES

We occasionally broke up into smaller groups in order to travel around in just one car. We visited various Cities and Counties. We sometimes were invited to be guests at various receptions. In the process we met lots of interesting people.

BLACK AND WHITE

I met two young married couples at a reception for us VISTAs in a small town. One couple was Black the other White.

The White couple said they went North for college for four years. They said the entire time they were there; White people just call them racist no matter what they said or did. They were forced to spend the bulk of their time with others from the South.

So, after they got their degrees they returned to North Carolina. They said the hatred was so prevalent in the North they knew there was no place for them. They were harassed because of their accents. They found that there was no changing the minds of the young liberals.

The Black couple explained to us they had gone north to an Ivy League college together. They said they were readily accepted by White people, especially in classes, study groups games, mealtimes, and the like.

However, when it came to things like birthday parties, Christmas holiday, travel, (anything really, very personal), they were never invited. They said they slowly realized what was going on re liberals and Blacks… behind the curtains.

They went on to say that when they returned to North Carolina they realized that they could trust the White people in North Carolina to tell the truth!

If they did not like you, North Carolina White people would tell or show you. If North Carolina White people said they liked you or tolerated you, they did.

What I got out of it was that in the North, basically White Liberals would say one thing to Blacks to their face, then often do something else with their actions. Southern Whites minced few words.

BLACK AND WHITE--- CHILDREN

Several of us were invited to attend/work at a day care center.

Mostly children in the 2-4-year-old age group.

Interestingly, it was a mixed-race group! Black and white children playing together… very nicely. A situation I had seldom witnessed back in Portland, though my cousin did attend a mixed-race kindergarten in the early 1950s. They learned their letters, colors and how to treat each other.

We played with them ourselves for about ½ hour. I was amazed at how I realized that blacks and whites were so much alike. This was a poorer area, so I had great hope for their futures with a good educational start like this!

MORE ON THE GROUND ASSIGNMENTS

We were generally relocated to other areas towards the Coast. We were probably within 20 miles of all the other VISTAs from our group.

We (my partner and I) first were assigned to a location near the City of Chinquapin, North Carolina. We were assigned to a very rural couple and their three children.

The adults had two somewhat attractive daughters, so (we presumed) they had us sleep in an out-building about 75 yards down the road.

The girls, one 14 and one 16 attended a local high school and attracted lots of boys. Several high school boys would drive by and stop almost daily. The 16-year-old was a tall blond athlete. But it was her 14-year-old sister who attracted the most boyfriends. She was, ahem, somewhat more developed than her older sister.

The two sisters had a brother, who was mildly retarded. He was a hard worker but not a deep thinker. He had a tough time with conversations AND was manipulatable.

For instance, a local farmer stopped by and asked him if he would

work for him the next morning. He confessed he forgot and that he would be working for someone else.

The farmer said he would be forced to hire a Negro (we were standing right there) if he could not work for him and begged him to show up. The brother reluctantly agreed and the farmer, with a smirk on his face, said he would pick him up in the morning.

The parents could best be described as "three miles" people. In other words, from birth tile now, they had never gone more than a few miles from their place of birth. So, they enjoyed any trips we could provide.

We drove ourselves and often our "parents" around as well as ourselves to explore the County. We hit a few local cities and stores they had never visited.

FISHING TRIP

My roommate and I decided to take a fishing trip deep down into a swamp that started just out back of our residence.

We bought fishhooks, lines and figured we would just cut fishing poles from swamp trees.

When we got to the swamp and then deep inside, we baited the hooks, tied the lines to our poles (branches we had cut to about 6 feet) and began to fish. We spent nearly an hour fishing getting several bites, but it seems the fish were smarter than we were.

But, as we walked around, in one area we discovered "something" hanging by a string over the water from a branch. Below it there were tons of maggots and then fish coming up from the bottom going after them.

While we surely could have caught some fish, it turned out that the "something" hanging from the limb was an exceptionally long and large snake, about 3 feet long. It was slit down the middle. We took one look and ran on out of there!

We went fishing on the Cape Fear River a little later in the year with some other VISTAs. There just was not anything biting then. I did show some folks how to make makeshift rafts and sail along the shore of the one open beach we could find.

It was a lot of fun, but we all got well soaked. The water was cool, but the beach was blazing hot. Choices were not really there for us citified folks!

GREAT BALLS O' FIRE.

On a day later that week, we came back early from our VISTA meeting. We said "hello" to the folks and went back the few yards to our place.

While wandering/sitting around our little room, we heard the weather pick up like it occasionally did in the afternoons. The wind was blowing strong. We also started getting some rain, not uncommon either.

Then off in the distance we heard an increasingly loud BOOMING/ROARING type noise. We both looked out our front and only window. When we looked, we saw a huge ball of light or fire or something coming right down the road passing by the front of our place! It made a deafening roar as it went past and on down the road.

We watched it as it hit a large Silo off in the distance. We heard chunks of the Silo plus some parts of surrounding buildings being knocked off/out into the nearby area. And the fire ball kept on going away from us!

We had no idea what it was. Just some kind of giant ball of flames... perhaps a missile or bomb or something. But that did not seem to make any sense.

Suddenly - it dawned on me that it MIGHT have been a "GREAT BALL OF FIRE" a phrase I had always attributed to being something in the South, but I never understood it.

We ran next door to check on the folks. They were out front and saw it coming and ran in their side door - just as it blew by. They said they saw them every couple year or so. They were quietly amused at our display of shock and fear.

We got in our vehicle and drove on down the road toward where the BALL of FIRE headed. We saw the remains of the Silo and a few buildings down its path. It had gone in a very straight line so nothing to the left or right of it was damaged. It was a scary experience to say the least!

Later we found out their kids were all gone that afternoon and so did not see it. But they said they too had seen them in the past- which means they must have been somewhat common out there!

REVIVAL

One Saturday night the mother told us she was going to a REVIVAL Meeting. She said she and a lady friend regularly attended them together, usually monthly.

She added that there would be a "gen-u-in" Minister with all the works! She was overly excited and got dressed up real nice. She later got picked up by her friend who "carried" her on out of there.

The next morning when we saw her, her hair was cut, noticeably short! She explained that the preacher at the Revival said the devil was giving her evil thoughts through her hair and he offered to and did cut her hair... near bald! That apparently removed those thoughts.

Her family was a bit perturbed and scared but supported her and said nothing... in front of us.

ENTERTAINMENT

On Sunday nights when Bonanza was on, we drove them to their friends who had a TV. This was a huge treat for them. They knew all the Cartwrights by their peculiarities. Who was afraid of snakes, liked which foods, the whole list of them? They were very ardent fans! The next couple of weeks we just dropped them off and picked them up.

Our DEPARTURE FROM THE FAMILY

After three weeks we got ready to leave the family. We owed them $50 per week for each of us. On the Saturday before our departure we sat the mother down and then paid her $50 per week for the three weeks apiece for a total of $300. Her eyes rolled back in her head and she almost fainted. She said nothing but left the room with the money.

The next day, Sunday, she fixed us the finest Southern Meal we had ever had, before or after. Chicken, grits, biscuits, the works.

We left the family on a Wednesday. It was incredibly sad. I really liked those people. I hated the situation we and they were in, but they were great people.

The dad, despite his shortcomings had a sense of humor even with all he had gone through. He remembered things that are worth remembering and he noticed the little things.

We were sad to say goodbye BUT we knew more VISTAs would be staying with them in the future. We did visit again and met the two guys who had moved into the little shack we had. These VISTAs loved the people and place as much as we did!

FINAL VISIT WITH THE FAMILY

At a much later date, and truly our final visit, the mother invited us in, and we saw the girls, brother, dad all watching TV. They barely acknowledged our existence.

The younger girl's boyfriend bought them a TV (just before he entered the Service) and mom said that is all any of them did anymore.

She said they just sat there watching program after program. She sounded disgusted to say the least and it did appear to be what had happened throughout the rest of the US in the 1950s when TVs first hit it big.

We said our final "goodbye" to the mother (and waved goodbye to the others) and noted mom's look of disgust as she had lost her family to the "Boob Tube."

NOTE: I did return to the area some twenty years later. Their house was gone and there was nothing around there to identify it had ever existed.

No house, trees, or anything. It was all tobacco land then.

VISITING WITH OTHER VISTAS

We spent a lot of time going from City to City (small towns). Most if not all people we met were friendly. They would listen to our story of why we were in their state. We often got invited by a mayor or County official to an official get together! We would meet a council or other group of elected people.

I recall going to a small house near a military base. There was a Black couple living in it. I explained what I was doing. They replied they were new there themselves and had never seen such abject poverty, regardless of race.

They asked how they could help and sadly I had to say I did not know anything about the local processes or procedure. Just stated they should go to the local Social Services Office to volunteer. Also suggested they keep on the lookout for a permanently stationed VISTA.

REPAIRMAN

Interestingly, few of the other VISTAs I met, knew how to fix anything. By that I mean they could not work on a car or even repair any home appliances.

I had to show a couple guys how to take out and install a rebuilt starter motor, which amazed them.

In another case I went to help a couple guys repair their toilet. Their water bill was over $100 a month, which was astonishing to me! I asked them why. They said they didn't know anything, but the water just kept running. They could turn it off and on with the handle at the base of the toilet but that was tough to use.

So, I took off the toilet lid and saw that parts of the innards had come apart thus allowing the water to keep running. I realized it just needed to be reattached. I fixed it in about ten minutes. The water stopped running and they thought I was Mechanical Genius!

PET?

Two Vistas decided to buy a baby crocodile! It was neat. They built a little island in one of those little plastic sided portable pools and put him in there. It stayed in it and was well fed. It was so well fed it grew rapidly. Each time we came by it seemed to be another inch or two longer.

For a month or so it was fun for us and them to feed and play with it. But after the second month it got bigger and its bites began to hurt!

So, after much discussion, we/they took a road trip with it and released it into a swamp down towards South Carolina. It was painful thing for them to do, but it was the safest and most righteous thing for them to do.

PULLED OVER

The same two older VISTAs also got pulled over by the infamous NC State Patrol (Wolf Pack, back then).

These two had earlier stopped at a café to have lunch. They took out some Turkish Cigarettes they had bought and told everyone in the little restaurant they were smoking Marijuana Cigarettes. They pretended to get high and the rest of it. They made a pretty loud and obnoxious scene, just wanting to play with them.

The State Patrol pulled them over on the way out of there. They were surrounded with guns drawn on them. The State Patrol explained why they were being pulled over and asked them if they had any Marijuana on them or in the car or anything.

During questioning they explained and showed them their "Marijuana" Cigarettes, the Turkish Cigarette packs, and the rest. They explained they were just messing with the locals and were deeply sorry they had done it.

The State Patrol explained they should not do things like that as this wasn't the big city and it upset the locals. The two promised never to do it again, so the State Patrol just let them go- without searching their car.

They laughed and sort of cringed at the same time. They told us they actually had Marijuana under their front seat and would have been arrested and jailed for having so much!

They were able to bluff their way through it all and laughed, on and off, plus some personal screaming to themselves, for a week or so.

DOWN THE CAPE FEAR RIVER

These two same guys decided to take a boat/float trip down the Cape Fear River in Eastern North Carolina. They bought their boat and all their equipment, including sleeping bags, netting, and a gas stove. They made out a detailed plan for where they would start out and how they would get picked up at the end.

They especially noted they planned on tying up along the river's shore each night.

They then discussed their proposed trip with our local County VISTA Director. He said it sounded fine, but he asked if they had plans for snakes that might drop down from limbs at night. Without much discussion they cancelled the trip altogether and concentrated on camping on wide sandy beaches- with cots!

SOUTH CAROLINA ROAD TRIP

Five of us took a road trip to South Carolina. On the way down, we stopped at a little roadside grocery store. The owner asked us what we were doing. We explained what we did and who we tried to help.

He said one thing he observed was extremely poor people, black and white, buying laundry starch. He said he believed/had heard they were mixing it with flour to make some kind of pancake type mix.

He thought it was not good for people to eat but they seemed to want it because it went a long way. Most of these folks had children so it is tough to imagine what the long-term effects were.

The owner said there really was nothing he could do about it except tell people like us. We suggested he contact local authorities, but we have no idea if he did or not.

SWAMP LAKE

On this same trip we <u>un</u>eventfully stopped at a stop sign. Off to the left there was a small stream coming out of a swamp like area. Under the trees I could see a large pond. There was a dock, with someone fishing off it.

There was a lone light bulb hanging down from a tree limb above the dock. It was lighting everything up.

Off to one side, a boat floating, tied to the dock. I could never forget this and have paid people to paint it!

BREAKING AND ENTERING

We (probably 5 of us VISTAS) snuck into lots of old abandoned homes/buildings in the area around where we all met.

The depression of the thirties drove lots of people out of the small towns. And new jobs (Union jobs) in the North in the 50s and 60s called them out as well. They could make nearly twice as much money up North as they could in the Carolinas.

We heard some people took TWO shifts at auto factories in Detroit so they would get double pensions in twenty years. Some of them were already retiring on their pensions!

We broke into a few places. Actually, they weren't locked or even barricaded. We would see, get curious then walk right in.

First place was a Russian Orthodox Church. Pews, altar, side altars, statues, all untouched since the last service… we presumed.

There was a leak in the ceiling above the main altar and rainwater had done considerable damage. The top of the altar was completely messed up with the sides somewhat rotted out. The floor was also damaged and water leaked into the basement...

There were lots of BINGO cards lying around, sort of like a good Catholic Church.

The basement was loaded with old fashioned (to me) desks and chairs.

Looked like it was a school unto itself. Chalkboards, chalk and the rest were spread around the area.

We did no damage, but our photographer couple took great "as is" photos. Again, the only damage appeared to be from the elements to the altar.

We went to <u>another place</u>, kind of a Ranch style home. Letters we found just strewn about the house, indicated the people there had left in the mid-1950s to move North. They noted they sought more economic opportunity. The house was quite tired looking inside and out.

No one had ever maintained any of it after the owners left, but it was not ransacked or damaged. It just sat there. They were not resold or occupied, we were told, because the people just abandoned them. With so many moving North, there was not much chance of selling them.

The third place required us to use some flashlights as it was night-time. There was an active homestead about a quarter mile down the road, but no one ever bothered us.

It was a very old house, abandoned in the early 1900s, probably 1910. There was a painting of Napoleon Bonaparte on a wall next to a cracked long mirror. It was a great view and extremely photogenic.

And there were plates and serving dishes on the main table with what appeared to be food scraps still on them! The dining room and the rest of the house looked like someone was sitting there then suddenly got up and abandoned it all. Everything was just sitting there.

The couple took hundreds of great photos over the year they were in NC. Never heard what they did with the photos.

We never got caught in any of those places. I can recall breaking/sneaking into other places but have no specific recollections.

THE END OF THE BEGINNING

Finally, we all had to go through an evaluation at a major meeting. Mainly they wanted to see if we still wanted to stay in the program.

One girl was let go and I never knew why. Most of us wanted to stay/leave.

We were and had met people of all ages, genders, demeanors, and interpersonal skills.

The final evaluation left most of us with mixed feelings. We got selected to stay though several of us were not sure we wanted to stay. Our futures were too uncertain.

Eventually we survivors were teamed up into pairs and sent off to different small-town locations.

PART IV

THE NEXT STEP

In September, on a Tuesday, those of us who survived the six plus weeks of training/experience, were asked to become official Vista Volunteers. They walked around asking each of us if we were ready, etc. to put in a full year.

A few contemplated spending 10 more months there and just left. A few more were rejected as they just did not appear to want to be there or didn't "get" what they were supposed to do.

Those of us who were left were given a little card saying we were: OFFICIAL VISTA VOLUNTEERS!

We later got little pins for our shirts, which were very officious appearing, though some of us only wore them when visiting official offices and NOT real people!

FINAL ASSIGNMENTS

We were also assigned to our final assigned places. We were told where we would be working and who we would be partnered with. Despite the fact we all moved into different cities, they held biweekly meetings so we could meet and share information. This really helped keep us all on task.

I was assigned to work with my former roomie Kent. He and I hit it off well before and when we worked together. So, it was a no brainer.

Kent and I were sent to a nice, small town. It had about 10,000 citizens. It was between other cities of about 10,000 citizens. In fact, North Carolina had some 100 cities of 10,000 or more people, largest number of similar sized cities of any US State!

On our first day in town, we started looking for a place to stay. We were told the local Police Department could find us a place to stay which they did. We got a fairly nice place for about $45 per month not including utilities.

It had lots of mice and some rats. It used to be the farmhouse for the corn and wheat fields surrounding us. The owners moved into a nice new place and rented this one out.

It had a huge front room and a large kitchen. The bedrooms were small. It had a combination bathtub/shower, a rarity then.

It had gas heat but everything else was electric. We split the $45 monthly rent. We got this place the first day we arrived.

On Thursday we somewhat furnished it for $100. A kitchen chair and another chair. They cost $25. A refrigerator was $30, stove $30, chest and drawers $15. We borrowed mattresses from other Vistas until we got enough money to buy more furnishings.

I ran into a local politician in the downtown area. We were discussing crime and other problems. He said one issue they have is how they process car registration as well as car Insurance.

He said you cannot get a license plate unless you first have insurance on the car. That stopped a lot of untrustworthy people from buying.

He explained that lots of people STEAL license plates off cars and simply swap them out every month or so. He said that way they always had a new one. I explained I had never heard of that. We both then went about our business.

We went to a Military Base along the coast to buy furniture for our household. It was a military auction with most people spending a fortune on junk.

Never forget one guy spending $125 on a pool table where the slate top was shattered and was merely pieced back together. He himself could not believe what he had done, admitting he got carried away.

We bought lamps and other small furnishings, things we could haul back in our Government Vehicle.

BLACK RESIDENTS

Along with visiting other Blacks, I recall going to a small house near a military base. There was a Black couple living in it. I explained what I was doing. They replied they were new there themselves and had never seen such abject poverty, regardless of race. They asked how they could help and sadly I had to say I did not know anything about the local conditions and the people running the area. I suggested they keep on the lookout for VISTAs and the local Social Services Agencies. (Not much help!)

NEIGHBOR

A neighbor lady stopped by and offered to bake us a Pecan Pie if we mowed her lawn. We jumped at the chance, did it that afternoon, including raking and piling the remains. The pie, with some whipped cream, was delicious!

She asked us to do it and accepted a couple more times before the Fall.

COSTS

A local store allowed people to run up tabs. While I was standing in the checkout line, one Black couple asked for a status of their bill. The clerk stated it was "only" 30 or so bucks. It was a tremendous amount for them, and they looked at each other in disbelief. They made a partial payment and left.

Good news was that more and more larger stores were coming into the City and this one was bound to go under. But in the meantime, this was one of the few stores where poor people could get credit.

Very rural. We went to a local theater and it was segregated by cost. Blacks took the Lodges up above because they were 20 cents cheaper and we Whites stayed on the main floor. It was the way that segregation, to a degree, continued. We went only the one time because of the way we felt in the All-White area.

GOVERNMENT VEHICLE

While it was 1968, I did get assigned an older FBI car converted for VISTA use. It was a 1964 Dodge Charger. Never knew what it had under the hood until one afternoon on a freeway when I realized I could not get it out of second to third gear.

I pulled over and looked under the hood. When I did, I could not believe the size of the engine. It was an absolute monster- the largest one they made back then. It came with a tremendous amount of HP.

After getting over that I checked the transmission. It quickly became apparent the linkage for 3rd gear had given out. After finding the part that had given out and tightening it, I was able to get it to working again.

I floored it and it took off like a cannon.

It was great. I ruled the roads for a good month or so until I bought my own car as noted above and returned the beast to the local Agency.

(We did not like the government vehicles because they identified us as Government Employees which was frowned upon back then- by both Blacks and Whites.)

SURPLUS GOVERNMENT FOOD

Back in those days the Federal Government provided food for the needy. It got sent to social services agencies. They would box it up and take it to local needy people.

One time I helped them unload a truck full of the food to the Agency dock. It was 17 tons of every kind of surplus food you could imagine.

Cheese, corn meal, oats, various dried and canned foods as well as various vegetables.

I went with the Social Workers to deliver to several homes. It was quite an education.

The folks often did not use the grains for what was proposed. They might use oat grains to feed their chickens. Cheese might be sold to neighbors.

Turns out a lot of opportunity was given to the Social Workers and their Aides. They were given the opportunity to visit with and teach the mother things about running a household.

I recall one place where there was a small child lying on its back on a blanket on a mattress. The child was cooing and staring at us. The Social worker Aide later told me the mother was struggling to buy clothing and that even diapers were in short supply.

The mother thanked us profusely as we headed on out to the next and similar place.

ROOMIE AND I TRUDGING AROUND A TOWN

We started to head out to both Black and White parts of a local town. We simply walked from door to door. (Most people might recognize us from Church or the downtown area-but all treated us well). Most had to turn down a tv as they came to the door.

After explaining who we were, handing out literature, etc. we just asked questions about the kinds of work/ jobs, what do you do for fun, any major events around here, and even more etc.

We might hit 20 shops or homes a day, depending on what time we were there. Most men had some kind of job, with women often at home with the kids or dealing with their school or family matters.

Some places/people, especially farmers, wanting to hire Black or White right away. Lots of kids were moving North then.

Farming of course was a business that required a lot of hands on labor. It might not last for long, but it was steady when it was steady. And, at the least it was work.

COUNTY OFFICIALS

We also went to the local County Offices. One County ushered us right into one of their meetings. They were in the midst of voting on and discussing various matters. They were all men with one female note taker.

We introduced ourselves and they said we could talk. So, we explained VISTA and what our goals etc. were.

When we were done with our near off the cuff presentation, we asked if anyone had any questions. The men looked at each other and no one had anything to ask.

But the well endowed blond-haired woman taking notes did start asking us questions. She was the County Clerk and meeting note taker.

"Was our plan to stir things up, did we have proper credentials, how long would we be there, would we be talking to Blacks, how come local people couldn't do this?"

We were able to answer all her questions aggressively as well as completely, thankfully. It was amazing how curious about us and VISTA she was vs how accepting the elected folks were. In my opinion she should have been the Lead County Commissioner to say the least.

Anyhow, we never got confronted or mistreated by anyone. Most just answered our inquiries then thanked us for stopping by.

NORTHWARD MIGRATION IN 1968

This was at a time when younger people were moving north- both Black and White. There was factory work in the North and Northeast and that drew a lot of the young there.

That began a slight labor shortage in some areas around here. Ironically, one of the biggest complaints we got from the poor, again Black and White, were lack of more and better paying jobs.

No one of any color or race wanted to discuss race or racism or anything like that with us. We might have seemed too threatening or something.

CHURCHES

On one fine Sunday we went to a Black Baptist Church. It was closing in on November, election time. The Minister was talking about the upcoming election (Nixon/Humphry). BUT he noted he could not state any preference because he couldn't campaign in Church.

But the minister stated that, while he could not campaign in Church (everyone looked at us with big smiles), he said he knew who HE was voting for and hoped everyone else did. Everyone looked at us and cheered and clapped, as did we!

As it was approaching Christmas, a lot of the songs sung were Christmas themed. They sang deeply and meaningfully to say the least.

All Churches were very segregated. However, despite the segregation, Black and White churches had pretty much the same ceremony.

We seemed to cause consternation in both but eventually both acted as if we were not there. Lots of "halleluiahs" and confessions of faith and the like in both.

Some people would confess sins or step to take Jesus into their lives. Very emotional to say the least. Mostly the ministers would shake our hands as we left. Few Parishioners did. We never saw them again.

(If only they would have gone to each other's churches they would have easily seen that they had so much more in common than not).

CATHOLIC CHURCHES

We attended one Catholic Church because it was NOT segregated, though there were very few Black Catholics in attendance.

We asked how in the heck they ended up with Catholics in the South. Someone explained a famous

Archbishop was traveling up the coast and stopped at a few places to preach.

He decided to head inland a hundred or so miles to this area and convinced the locals of the value of Catholicism. He did so by preaching, long, hard, deeply, emotionally and managing to attach to them.

I still could NOT figure how a Catholic could get anywhere in a Baptist area. Black Baptists would have received more approval than a White Catholic, or so it seemed.

But the Catholics were in a geographically small area so maybe there was not anyone else there. There were Catholic grade and high schools to boot.

SLIPPERY ACCENTS

I did meet a State politician. I was coming out of a small store with my VISTA Pin very visible. Turns out he was a State Representative from Raleigh out on an information tour.

At first, he spoke with a plain, almost midwestern type accent. But as we spoke his real and Southern accent slowly returned. I noticed all sorts of people, even Blacks, had "slippery" accents that might change over the course of a conversation.

(I also liked to ask the Native North Carolinians what and where they thought Oregon was. The closest anyone got was: "where all that logging goes on." Otherwise, Black, or White, they knew that it was somewhere near California or nothing at all).

Dining Out. We occasionally ate out at local restaurants. The food was good but most importantly the prices were low!

I got used to "hominy grits and corn pones. " They were great Southern

Dishes. I really missed them when I left.

They were a particularly "Southern Dish" back then. When I got back to Portland, Oregon I could occasionally find grits, but not often- and they were not nearly as good. Not as salty/greasy, I guess.

I never found corn pones though I did not look as hard. Soon I forgot them both, dang it.

OTHER PLACES

During the day we mostly went into local towns, introduced ourselves to City/County officials and then the police. We wanted to make ourselves known up front rather than via rumors!

One place we stopped in had a coal or other type mine that had closed. The town took a huge economic beating. High unemployment then, even though it had closed, slowly, starting a couple years before. We heard a lot about the mine even then and how few other jobs paid as much.

Also, a couple factories had closed down. No matter how low the pay or demeaning the work might be described, they were jobs that paid better than farm work.

There were also some new to the area factories/jobs. Several companies had moved from the North to take advantage of the cheaper labor and smaller tax burdens.

Despite the fact we were pretty much separated from the other VISTAs, we were able to travel and meet with them as often as we liked, and we did.

BLACK LIVES CHANGING

There was a trend in the State toward kids, especially Black ones, getting a high school diploma. I emphasize the word "trend" because it was not quite widespread- as hoped by their mothers.

Too many kids quit simply because they could not handle the material. Their home life often did not support their school life and they fell behind and got discouraged.

Black mothers wanted what was best for their boys (and girls though they were already working hard and taking advantage of the more inclusive education system). They pushed and prodded them both.

As noted above, however, more and more youth, especially Blacks, were moving North for jobs and other opportunities. Education was becoming less necessary and less valuable… as I was told.

HO-HUM-ERY

Our work and challenges were slow, for a while, thus we had a lot of time on our hands. We spent a lot of time at our house, just observing what was occurring in nature.

Coolest thing we experienced were Black and Brown birds in the local field behind our place. Farmers had harvested the corn, but the residue attracted what seemed like MILLIONS of birds.

One time they were flying by us and landing and moving on. It went on for nearly 30 minutes. Nothing we did or threw interrupted their assault on the fields. It was memorable to say the least.

SMALL TOWN

While walking around YET another small town, we were on the lookout to meet local citizens. We also wanted to know where people went in this little town.

We checked with a few Black folks, mostly ministers and some teachers. They pointed out the restaurants and even where we could get haircuts, which we did.

One Saturday we decided to drive to and into yet another small City. There was a major park in the middle of town. We went to the park expecting to see lots of kids/people playing but there were few. We were stunned and after about 20 minutes we upped and moved on.

We talked to a Black grocery clerk later and he told us that it used to be a major mostly White park. Blacks could only go when Whites were not there or Sundays. It was like that for decades. It took Federal legislation to change it.

But when civil rights laws occurred allowing Blacks to be there at the same time, Whites quit going. And when Whites quit going, Blacks said "we won't go either."

And so, for the brief time we were there it was not used by either race, at least on weekends. I have no idea how long it took to move past that behavior.

A local White grocery store clerk told us that clerks at some stores cheat mostly poor Blacks but some Whites as well. He said they would process all the goods the customer put on the counter but would occasionally slip a dummy one in and then hide it away when done. I had never heard of that up to then but asked other people about it and indeed it occurred in more than one store.

The main all White High School was already integrated, to some extent. Probably had 40-50 Blacks vs 300 White children.

This was approaching election time in 1968. The White Principal explained his students were acting just like their "adult" counterparts had done earlier in Chicago. In his school both races were rioting, screaming about unfairness, etc.

Most schools were somewhat integrated. Interestingly mostly White schools had Blacks on their sports teams. And they were well received. Like so many places in the US, racial mixing was often first started/accepted by athletes!

Another Principal also noted when he was growing up, they played with Black kids just like with other White kids. He said the exception was they did not go to each other's homes. (same issue my Swiss born mother faced when she grew up in the US in the 1920s when meeting "True" Americans).

The all Black school at the other end of town was run by a Black Principal. He was not helpful regarding race relations. He was mostly interested in getting us to rent one of his mobile homes on his school grounds. He was not helpful in us learning about the community.

We found the City very segregated, especially by housing. We did run into an old plantation type house, very classic. There was a small White child playing on a swing in the back yard. A very fierce "Black Nanny" stood protectively over her, glaring at us, as we walked by.

There were separate Black and White parts of the City. We got haircuts at a Black shop just into the Black side of town. Everyone seemed uptight and anxious while we were there, like they were waiting for the other shoe to drop! But the barbers cut our hair and the price was right…just a little tense!

Interestingly, last names of residents we met were often the same for Blacks and Whites. I believe Black slaves had taken on the last name of their owners, but I could not confirm that.

If true it would have been an interesting phenomena to deal with: "My daddy's daddy's daddy used to own your daddy's, daddy's daddy- I imagined."

Elsewhere we saw a White woman selling REVLON or some such product. She pulled up in front of a house, honked her horn and a Black lady came out with money and went up to the car window and gave the lady money in exchange for some product. The White lady never got out of her car. They both glared at us.

HATFIELD VS MCCOYS??

(or segregation with nothing to do with race)

We had to pick up some lumber and asked around. Everyone recommended this place at the far end of town. The clerk working there was the daughter of the owner. She was drop dead gorgeous. We bought some items but went back a couple more times… just to uh, you know.

It was a real well operated saw and lumber mill. They cut the rough lumber they got into various sizes and shapes. Their product was perfect.

However, a local store clerk said that the funny thing was where they bought their rough lumber. We had no clue, but he was interested in telling us.

He said there was a nice log mill at the far end of town. But the lumber mill we went to get their material from about 20 miles away. The two White owned businesses located at opposite ends of the town, didn't do business with each other.

They went to a lot of trouble to avoid each other. He said the two families started feuding about 1910 and hadn't spoken or dealt with each other since!

PRINCIPLES

Another case of that was of a White Principal who explained his problems. While he had been principal for some 15 years there were some things he couldn't get right. He said when he selected people to work on the Christmas Committee, he always had to run it by his receptionist.

The receptionist was born in the City and knew everyone, especially those

who were getting along with whom.
The Principal said this year was
particularly good for him because he
only selected a couple of people to be
on the same committee who weren't
talking to each other right then. He
said if he hadn't had it checked out, it
would have been a disaster! He
remarked that that was the way it was
in that town.

FUN

We asked some Black teens what they
did for fun around there. They told us
about a "PICCALO JOINT." They told
us that kids would go there to party,
drink pop, etc.

They pointed to where it was and ran
off. Not knowing any better we went
down there.

All the Blacks we came across there,
and in the area, began to walk or run
away as we approached. We

innocently walked into the PICCALO JOINT and the place cleared out.

We figured SOMETHING was going on in there and it probably wasn't too innocent. We finally just left. We never did figure out what happened there.

CIVIL WAR MEMORY
(A trip that answered some questions)

Interestingly my Roomie and I decided to drive to an old Civil War Site where some battle or other was fought. We thought it was strange to keep such a place like that.

We went in, saw the memorial and then the actual site itself. It was laid out, marked, generally where people had died. I dug up a bullet myself.

But after a while, a weird feeling came over both of us. We got a sense that something REAL had happened there. We had visions of death but honor, bravery, and more death!

I ever after understood why there were such things as CIVIL WAR reenactments. People fought bravely on both sides and never lost this feeling. This stuff never went away.

To this day I see the Civil War as more than just a series of battles! And with some 5,000 blacks fighting for the South I could understand why some reenactments had blacks involved.

KKK?

We also were driving along when we saw a dirt/grass covered road taking off to the right. We decided to follow the road, as long as it was decent. We went about a mile up the road until it opened to a grassy field about a half-acre in size, surrounded by trees.

We stopped and looked at it all especially the pole in the middle, though there was no sign of fires or burning or anything. We soaked it in for a while, then realized it MIGHT have been a KLAN meeting place! We got out of there as fast as we could and never looked back. We discussed it with other VISTAs, and they said while it might have been a Klan place there was no really telling.

BUYING OUR OWN CARS

After being in North Carolina for a few months or so I decided to buy a car. For $300 I was the proud owner of a dull blue1962 Ford Fairlane!

I bought it on a hot day and I never bothered to roll up the window. When the weather got colder, and I tried to roll the window up, it turned out the glass inside the window frame was broken!

The handle would turn … but it just never grasped onto anything! You could hear glass rolling around inside as the little wheels turned. I never went back to the guy and just took it as a lesson well learned.

My roommate bought a 64 convertible, Corvair. In 1968 it was rightfully called: "Unsafe at any speed."

But, despite the fact he had trouble starting it, it was a great car. My wreck was able to go further distances between breakdowns, but both did get us around to those places you didn't want to get caught in a Government vehicle!

I eventually took it to a local repair shop, an event which had lessons galore. A short, thin black guy worked on my window. He was very conscientious with his work. He took the inside of the door out then took all the broken glass out. He measured the window (he didn't have a Ford Manual) and created an outline of what it should look like, using the right-side window for more precise measurements.

He then laid the outline on a piece of glass. He traced, marked, and cut everything in the most precise way. He took the glass and fit it in and anchored it to the inside of the window casing and soon I had a new left front window!

The VERY LARGE HULKING white guy and he bantered back and forth about race, filled with righteousness, etc. as they worked on their own separate projects.

The most interesting thing was that the White guy was putting new covers on one of someone's car seats. He was huge but he was able to do the dainty work it required. The work required delicacy and he had it! It was interesting to watch.

They continued to bicker as I paid up and got ready to leave. The dealer noted I was almost out of gas and asked the black guy to give me a couple gallons to get me to a gas station.

BUT the Black guy gave me 10 gallons and noted it on their books as two gallons. He winked at me just before he angrily stormed back to the garage.

Their bickering reminded me of the bickering the Police in Charlotte did a while earlier.

As I left, I noted it was an interesting set of circumstances. They were getting their feelings out of their systems- probably those that come from working with someone you were not used to. And these feelings appeared very mutual.

DEAD DOG

One night we were driving along an old, darkened road in his Corvair, probably 40 miles per hour. Out of nowhere, a pack of about 6 dogs came running across the road in front of us. Before he could do anything, we hit a very large dog.

We immediately stopped and got out. The dog was lying on the ground dead. We then heard voices and decided to get out of there!

We jumped back in the car and he started to start it. It would turn over but not start, what it often did when warmed up. The voices got louder and closer and angrier as his cart finally came to life!

We got out of there with probably just seconds to spare. We felt bad but it was probably a smart thing to so under the circumstances.

OTHER CONTACTS DURING the PROCESS

Another local Social Worker I met, a Black guy, was talking about his mother as he drove us through the city (He had just purchased a new Mustang in Detroit. It was fast and gorgeous). Today it would be worth a hundred grand!

His mother was being asked by the State, actually Social Services, to begin the process of going on Welfare.

He said that it was his childhood home and she did not want to move into public housing. He said the public housing they proposed was located along the river. Apparently, it was in a mosquito infested site– a terrible location.

So, we drove by the house and it was to me a ramshackle small place. There were several others just like it in the surrounding neighborhood.

I asked him what would become of her house. He said it would be taken over by the County and then auctioned off by the Sheriff. He said their goal was to revitalize that part of the City. I had not heard of such a thing and secretly assumed, despite the mosquitos, she would be better off near the river.

I went to another place with another social worker. It turned out to be a rugged, small log cabin with a dirt floor. The house sat on a five-acre parcel owned and occupied by a woman.

This lady was Native American, and the process was the same. Her 5-acre parcel was located on the side of somebody's 300 acre parcel. So, I was told, they wanted to move her out, in order to sell the property to the primary landowner.

We stopped and talked to her. She knew the Social Worker, so she invited us in to talk. She told us she was broke because her boyfriend was a cowboy and we should know how unreliable they are!

This is something I had not thought about, but being as people, were indeed on Welfare in the South – which I thought would be near impossible- as it was such a politically conservative area.

Right or wrong, I personally came to believe one of the main reason Welfare was allowed was to gain control over parcels of land and put people they didn't like (Black or White), into public housing units- out of the way.

Years later I recall reading when Black farmers were denied loans based on their skin color alone.

What I personally witnessed appeared to be the goal of just getting "undesirables" out of the way AND their properties into wealthier hands. Go figure.

VARIOUS ROAD TRIPS

Seeing Melvin Laird

Several of us got together and drove to Atlanta to hear Melvin Laird speak. During the beginning of his speech, the five or so of us were pointed out by Laird. The crowd of some thousands laughed at and ridiculed us.

It seemed kinda mean to us. After that I always figured I was probably on some kind of FBI list or other.

SIMON AND GARFUNKEL

On another occasion we drove to Duke University in the Summer of 1968 to see/hear Simon and Garfunkel. Several great pieces. Sometimes the audience was so deafening we couldn't hear the words… but no one cared.

At the end, one of them told us NOT to light matches when they sang the <u>SOUNDS of SILENCE.</u> They said the Fire Marshal frowned on that. So again, they repeated how upset the facility would be if we lit matches.

The auditorium was darkened, slowly and eerily. They began the song and as they continued, matches and lighters lit up. Even I, who didn't smoke had matches and joined in. It was a beautiful and spectacular song and experience. Doubt there was a dry eye in the house as we exited.

The whole event was wonderful. I had an album back home that had most of the pieces they played. It was unforgettable.

THE SMOKYS

Three of us decided to drive to the great Smokies near the North Carolina/Tennessee border. Since it was Autumn, we were told the leaves were changing color and were renowned to be beautiful. The whole experience would be unforgettable and life lasting.

We left on a Friday night and drove into the dark until we got close to the Park. We stopped at 3 AM. We slept until 5 am in the car and then drove on several more hours to the Park Entrance.

We got our Government Camping Permit and started walking. It was raining lightly but soon turned into a steady downpour.

While walking in, we got lost. The rain continued and we got heavily soaked. After an hour or more in the rain we finally found the cabin- which was a three-sided structure.

Fortunately, there was some dry wood in it. We cooked some food, got water, and set up our bed/cots with 3 blankets apiece.

The rain got heavier all the time until we could barely see out of our area - even with the flashlights. We then went to bed (bunk/cot). We fell asleep deeply as we were all exhausted and despite our best efforts, still a little hungry.

We were just about ready to fall into DEEP sleep when the sound of voices woke us up.

Six kids and 3 adults came in out of the rain into our little cabin! Their kids screamed. They were as surprised to see us as we were to see them.

After several minutes, we yelled trying to quiet them down. The adults tolerated us as we exchanged our Government Camping paperwork - showing both parties had the same cabin. Somehow the Government had screwed up royally.

So, the "adults" settled in after they quieted the kids down. They drank beer and laughed loudly. One of our party, indeed, wished he were Black, and we wondered what THEY would have thought if that were so.

They brought their own charcoal broiler. They kept it under the shelter roof towards our side of the cabin. We coughed and choked. Finally, one of us told them to put it out, which they did.

I just tried to sleep for the next few hours. At 11 o'clock they took to their bunks and went to sleep. At around 12:30 AM one of their kids screamed: "mommy, mommy! A bear, a bear!!"

Now this place was like Yellowstone, in that there were indeed plenty of bears around. So, no one, including me, laughed, or said anything. After a few seconds when nothing happened, he finally shut up

However, throughout the night he "spotted" bears 3 more times. The other kids eventually were laughing. It made for a long brutal night. The fathers were a little more patient than us. The other boys ridiculed the bear spotter, rightfully so, though he was probably terrified being where he was. He apparently was the "Leaders son", and he was the youngest appearing of the group, which made it tougher on the boy...

By 5 AM I was cold, hungry, and VERY tired. At 6 AM the "adults" got up and had the Cabin stoves and their gas stoves going while the kids were making tons of noise! So, we pretended to sleep during the chaos.

We got up around 8 and waited for them to move on. We left shortly after they did and went back to our car. We put our gear in the trunk and embarked on a nice long hike. The leaves were indeed beautiful, and the scenery was spectacular.

We then hiked back to my car. Naturally, it wouldn't start. We asked someone with a jumper cable for a "jump". They further helped us get it started. We then headed on out and onto the road.

On the drive back we did get to see some pretty scenery. We stopped at a small Creek. and walked over a bridge. We then followed a leaf covered path.

The trees were very colorful and beautiful. There were some long twine type "cables" going up the trees which we could swing on like Tarzan. We played with those for quite a while.

Soon after, we drove on until we found a picnic ground. We built a fire and cooked rice, soup, chicken in one pot. We then drove the couple hundred miles back home, stopping occasionally to enjoy the sights.

MISCELLANEOUS

Toward November, I started to come down with a sore throat. Historically for me that would lead to a cold followed by a flu like siege. BUT the weather, suddenly and mercifully, warmed up. It was warm enough to get me near symptom free in two days, a record for me.

JOE NAMATH

One of the VISTA girls made us spaghetti and meatballs the night of the famous Namath game of November 17, 1968. It looked like Namath was going to lose so the Network switched to the "Heidi" movie, so as to not disappoint the children.

The kids apparently loved it while we adults were disappointed. But we believed the Jets would lose, so it didn't hurt that bad—then.

However, Namath started catching the Jets up and we missed one of the greatest comeback games of all times. Grrr.

CHRISTMAS IN NEW YORK!

Just before Christmas, three of us went to New York City. Friends of mine, in a Volkswagen, drove us up there.

My NY friends (neighbor in Portland and his wife) wanted cartons of cigarettes from North Carolina, filter free. They had NO taxes on them in North Carolina, while New York had tons of taxes. So, I brought three cartons up with us.

We first went to the home of the parents of one of the other two VISTAS. We had dinner the one night we were there.

However, his grandfather, a grizzled old man, after hearing my name said: " The Irish may have built the transit system in New York, but it took the brains of the Jews to design them!" That quieted things down for a while, though I had no feelings one way or the other. It just seemed odd.

The next morning, we three went to my Portland friend's place in NY City. He and his wife were super appreciative for the Cigarettes. We chatted for a while, and, as it was early, we went to lunch.

My friend worked in welfare and told us all how he worked to keep the wrong people from getting on welfare. He singled out the Jews, several times. I was quietly embarrassed but sadly said nothing. My friends just stared at their food.

They left shortly thereafter, and it is when I told him they were both Jewish. He was pissed with me for not saying anything earlier. He soon got over it, though he was decidedly more careful regarding what he said in front of strangers!

(Interestingly, these two Jewish gentlemen and I disagreed

regarding the Arabs vs Israeli conflict. I believed that the Jews had taken the land rightfully in a war, from the Palestinians. They argued Israel was wrong to have kept it.

I argued that if the Israelis returned the land after that war, we might as well just abandon Israel to its own devices as they didn't really want to stay a nation. It never got to be a major issue, but it just was what it was.)

My friend's wife was a cab driver and had lots of interesting stories to tell. She was never robbed, never assaulted.

Lots of picking up drunks' stories and people not speaking much English.

They had one child, a little boy, (They had a wonderful Christmas planned for him which indeed came to pass). They had another on the way, a little girl!

Dave and I walked out Christmas Eve to get a Christmas Tree. He claimed that in NYC people got their trees very late in the season. As we walked around it turned out that most lots were either closed or had very few trees. Very few others appeared to be out looking for trees.

We did find one lot and we got a nice one fairly cheap. We got it to his place. He predicted his little boy would be very excited in the AM to see it (and he was).

I brought some gifts and they gave me some. The child was ecstatic with his. Very long, joyful morning and an excellent Christmas dinner.

The next night we went to their friend's apartment for a party. Lots of his friends were there. They spoke mostly about the various plays, movies they were in AND the numerous roles they were trying out for. Apparently, they had to go to place after place until they even got to audition then numerous more until they got a part.

I interjected that I didn't believe the plot for ROSEMARY'S BAB. It was my belief that no guy would sacrifice his wife and child for a mere movie role.

They all heartily laughed at me and basically said they would trade their mothers/souls for a decent part. I took acting a little more serious after that. I learned a lot that night!

SHUT DOWN

The third day I was there they told me they had to take the decorations down. He said they would need my help with the tree. Turns out it was going to cost them to get rid of the tree and decorations properly.

So, he dropped that plan. He said we would have to throw it out the window! We were only two stories up, but he insisted it would work.

So, we took all his wrappings, tree, and everything else and tossed it out around 1:00 am. Down it all fluttered to the sidewalk and steps below. What a mess.

When I went to leave the next morning, he said he would walk me to the bus depot. As we went out and down the steps, we could see all his tree, wreaths and other Christmas material lying along the sidewalk. He yelled out loud that some people have no respect for others or the City!

He got me to the bus depot and away I went for a good 8-hour trek. After several stops, I got dropped off right in front of my place. Just walked a few yards to my back door. Overall, it was one of the best vacation/trips I ever took or ever would. Did it all.

The next day I trekked around, drove around, killing time, waiting for my roommate to come back from his Christmas break. (I generally did not like going anywhere alone even in that small city). Turns out we BOTH had great Christmas holidays, though he got to go home.

INTERIM TRIP HOME TO PORTLAND

In another few weeks I would be heading home to Portland for two weeks to say hello and then goodbye again, to all. That too was a great trip.

I spoke at my Sister's high school, saw some of my lifelong friends and some relatives. Also went back to Montgomery Wards and Ireland's restaurant to see old workmates.

I finished up back at my old College to say one last "goodbye" to some old friends and some college professors.

It was a very intense and too short of a return trip that was tough to end.

PART V

JOBMO BILE

When I returned to North Carolina from my trip home in January, I was immediately transferred to Eastern

North Carolina to join/startup a program to be called: JOBMOBILE.

The goal of Jobmobile was to have someone go from place to place looking for people who were interested in work. The stops would be grocery stores, gas stations, wherever people might gather. They would be provided lists of jobs, receive assessments and perhaps providing them with training for various jobs.

Basically, the ultimate goal was to provide Employment Opportunities to the most rural of areas. It would also provide the opportunity to perhaps help reach people who currently were not receiving any Social Services.

On my way from the City to Henderson County in Western North Carolina, I stopped to get gas and some snacks at a little station/shop. I went in and noticed about 8 people milling around. The shopkeeper announced they were gypsies.

He loudly said they didn't bother him because Jesus was looking over him and his store. He pointed up toward the ceiling.

I could see there were windows around the inside walls where a person could see down. He said: "Jesus had a rifle and would protect him."

After thinking about the circumstances, I assumed there was someone up there walking around looking down- maybe with a rifle. I got out of there before anyone went crazy!

I arrived in a small City, proudly proclaiming itself to be: HENDERSONVILLE, the **Apple Capital of the World**. It was in Henderson County. (I later found there were some 8 other "Apple Capitals of the World in the US alone!)

My final venture began in midish January of 1969.

I would spend the next five-six or so months establishing and operating the program and keeping notes regarding how it was doing.

As noted, before it would result in a Report on what I did, <u>observed and suggestions I had to make it work.</u>

I reported to the local Social Services Office where I would be able to obtain the necessary information to enable me to proceed as well as deal with other matters.

I would need a Government Vehicle to look/appear official. Would also need a place to stay. I also needed a bank, and to figure out where things were.

The first few days I stayed at a motel. After that I moved into a place owned by an older Black gentleman, per the suggestion of the local Social Services office. He fixed breakfast and dinner when I needed them the two days I was there.

The second night I was there he invited me into his bedroom and asked me to step closer. He was in his nightgown and I got uncomfortable and left the room. I left the next day, telling the local Social Services Staff what had happened and what I suspected the guys intent was.

The next week I met another new guy. He told me he was planning on staying at that place. I told him what had happened to me. He looked at me like I was crazy and headed out to go over there.

The next time we were at a VISTA meeting, he explained he too had to leave - quickly- for the same reason.

BUT the office continued to place VISTAs in this place! Must have been an extreme shortage of places.

I drove/walked around the city for a couple of days. Eventually I went to a local newspaper office. It was closed. The drapes had been pulled back on the windows and I could see inside, but there was no one there.

I went to another Newspaper office. I told them what I saw and innocently asked if they were closed on Mondays. The guy said a couple months earlier the editor and several employees had taken some young girls up to a cabin in the mountains and had sex with them.

It was a HUGE unspoken scandal and we heard it nowhere else.

Apparently, they were not arrested, but they got caught. After having gotten caught they simply left the area and their families for a while. I never did follow up to find out what had happened and still don't know.

After living in several places, I met a couple guys who lived closer to where I wanted to be. The house they lived in was owned by an old gal named Floy Lyday. (Her house was/is in the background of the final scene of the movie: Thunder Road. It just flashes by, but it is worth looking at the old movie!)

In fact, in 1969 people vividly recalled the making of the Thunder Road in 1957-8. Lots of people got jobs. Lots of places got shut down for the road scenes though most of them were filmed in Tennessee or so we were told.

Several times the three of us we went to a local car racing track. Big, well lit, oval track, roaring engines, kind of cool. Very cool until the race was over and people hit the roads!

Lot of kids racing around. We only lived a couple miles away, so we didn't have much action ourselves.

But the kids raced around like it was Thunder Road all over again.

One eventful afternoon we spotted a fire up the hillside from us. A guy living up there had called the USFS to come fight it. We three got some hoses together and ran up to a guy's place and attached it to his house (He was OK with that). We started spraying the flames and hot spots when the USFS came over to us.

They told us to get the hose out of there because water was not putting the flames out below the surface. We started to protest but they were very adamant. So, we took them it away, disconnected it and brought them back to our place.

(Years later when I worked for the USFS I asked some of the fire fighters about the incident. They figured these guys were up to something else- but not efficient firefighting!)

We finally decided our place was too small and cramped. We began to look for another place and gave Floy Lyday a 30-day notice. As the days ran down, she came into our place more and more when we were gone.

One time she took all our empty beer, wine and whisky bottles and put them on the porch with several of our signs that basically said:

VISTA VOLUNTEERS HELPING OTHERS.

She then sent that photo to a local newspaper.

Our leader got word from the local newspaper of what had happened. We figured the worst. But we found out that one of the newspaper people was a SUPER DRUNK and they would not dare put it in the paper, as people would laugh at them for pointing fingers. So, we got away with it unscathed.

We eventually moved to another place nearby.

We moved to a three-room cabin on The Lake. One of us was devilishly handsome and he got the owners wife to rent to us at a reduced rate! Again, this was the engaged guy who only took advantage of his looks for things that benefitted us all.

So, the three of us moved to the Lake cabin for the last 4 months of my VISTA year.

MORE about the LAKE EXPERIENCES

By April, my final residence in North Carolina, was still on The Lake. We all would work the mornings and into the early afternoon, then head home in the afternoons and evenings.

One of our major stress relievers was DARTS! We could play for hours in the hot, humid days. We played 100, the one getting closest to 100 without exceeding it was the winner.

Of course, we always swam at the lake itself. There was a boat we could use to paddle around but often we just sat in the sun and/or flop into the water.

I could drink somewhat and if my stomach held out, I could get drunk!

The Sun/Heat was blazing hot despite the fact we were up 1,500 feet or so.

Towards April it began to rain fairly often. It would get hot, and then it would cloud up, then we would have a thundershower or two… per week.

These were often accompanied by hail. Sometimes the hail might take out portions of some crops or other. We sometimes drove around to see what damage might have occurred. Hail or the wind or whatever it was would cut fairly narrow 10-15-foot swaths through the rows of corn. It was educational to say the least.

CASINO

VISTA girls got invited to a local COVERT Casino. A local GENTLEMAN'S club invited any and all girls to go to the club to "gamble."

Wonder why just women? Anyhow they reported NO ISSUES with members, just lost some money.

MOONSHINE

A roommate had been out seeing some people and came back late. He woke us up and told us he had got us some MOONSHINE! He said it was from someone he was working with. I did NOT try any, but it smelled like Hell. Ugh.

He got pretty drunk off it- but there were no long term aftereffects we could see! (And surprisingly, the alcohol was crystal clear!).

We once tried to make our own moonshine. We took a lot of various fruits, added sugars, and put it in a small tank. Basically, it went sour so after a few miserable sips we threw it out!

One guy was making it in a small bottle which he put next to the kitchen sink. I had just walked away when it exploded. Apologies were profuse but it was memorable.

<u>VARIOUS EXPERIENCES</u>

We spent a lot of time traveling around. One time we were each assigned to a Social Service Worker. Our job was to go out and see what they did.

I got there late that morning and the only person left to go with was a hulking of a woman. Everyone else got the hotties, male and female.

So off we went. I asked her where we were going. She said we had to go and see if somebody was still pregnant! She said she was told the woman had had the baby, but it died. They fear the story is true and that she buried it somewhere around their home.

But now was lunch time and it was time to eat. We both brought sack lunches. She started talking about where we could park and eat.

She suggested a place called "Edge of the World." I agreed and so, there we went. We parked and walked about 200 feet from the parking lot up to a tiny park.

The park had tables where we sat and ate with a great view. Next to us there was virtually nothing! I walked over and looked over a cliff. There were no railings on the edge.

I could see out about five miles and all that was there were clouds. Down below the cliff there were some clouds covering the canyons (I guess they were canyons). It was the coolest thing I had ever experienced! She said it was her favorite place and I could see why.

We finished and we headed on up higher into apple country. As we drove along the winding road through the orchard, I saw someone look at us from behind some trees. Then they (he) just disappeared deep into the orchard.

We finally pulled up to a little house near the orchards. There was a blond-haired woman with two little kids on the porch. As we approached, the children ran on through the front door into the house.

The social worker, being very gracious and after identifying herself as a social worker, asked if we could go in and discuss things. The lady said" yes" so, in we went. The social worker chatted for a long time about anything other than the reason we were there.

I told the woman that I had seen someone in the orchard and the wife said it was probably her husband who is very, very shy.

The Social Worker finally, and without warning, asked the woman if she had been pregnant and if so where was the baby? The woman hemmed and hawed for a while and said nothing.

Then the Social Worker wrapped things up and said she would be out to speak with her again. She later explained that these things can't be rushed and that the hospital or her MD might have records, if they were involved. It was very stressful for the alleged mother, but she handled us well.

The main thing I got out of this was that, at the ripe old age of 23, I learned never, ever to judge someone by mere physical attributes. The SOMEWHAT

OBESE social worker was magnificent!

OTHER VISTAs

We also mingled with other VISTAs in the area though as the year played out, they were disappearing. Some VISTAs were not doing much. More and more, especially the women went back to their homes.

ASHVILLE NEWS ARTICLE

Saw an article in a local newspaper discussing why there were already TOO MANY JOBS in the Ashville area. They said if more companies moved in and hired people, UNIONs would be next. They claimed that what happened when there were unions… factories would close and move out of the area and jobs would disappear!

Policing. One of the many issues we were involved in, one of the more marked, was the failure of police to police in "colored towns." Police said the people will work it out for themselves… revenge. Blacks were very upset with that attitude.

In addition, one VISTA came back to our place at the Lake panicked. He said Blacks and Whites were squaring off for a fight. Police showed up and stood with the Whites!

What ensued was a "Beat Back" of the Blacks with no official inquiry into what was/had actually occurred. We only heard what happened as nothing appeared in the local newspaper or on the radio.

Interestingly the larger North Carolina cities had Blacks in their police departments. But they were then just beginning, slowly, to ensure justice for all.

PICTURES on the WALLS

Most of the resident homes we went into had pictures and photos on the walls. Most "White Homes" had both Franklin Roosevelt and John F Kennedy. Black homes always had Martin Luther King pictures as well.

HATE GROUPS?

In Eastern North Carolina it was the KKK. Here it looked like it was going to be more the John Birch Society, though the KKK was strong too. The Society had just begun informal investigations into just exactly what Vista was doing in their area.

They sent representatives to meetings to question us. Their classic line was: "What do you think of the people here?"

We VISTAs got together and worked out lines that would be acceptable.

One of the best was: "People are pretty much the same everywhere, etc."

Interestingly, when we stayed in an area for a period, people pretty much forgot about us … with some exceptions - in certain other parts of the State. We heard about some of our members being harassed or run out of an area but not frequently, though if it happened to you, it was enough!

BLACK AND WHITE Experience- and Education

One Black acquaintance I knew was telling us about how he and his wife were driving along a road when the NC State police pulled them over. They had him get out of the car, but his wife got mad and got out of the car and started threatening an officer.

The husband saw them put her face-first on the hood of the car. He got so mad he went into his car to get his gun that he always kept in the glove compartment - only to discover it wasn't there! They both were arrested/taken in but then released.

He looked off into space while telling us this anecdote, and said, in a wondering way... **"how different his life might have been had the gun been there."**

CIVIL WAR

Later I went to one very small town where many folks were descendants of Civil War deserters. VERY isolated town and tough to find even in the 1960s.

It was high up in the mountains, no school, few kids anyhow. We just drove through, no paved roads, very old homes, and buildings. Not particularly a tourist place!

NOT HELL BUT CLOSE TO IT

Another area we went through was called PURGATORY ROAD due to the high number of people with genetic disorders. Extra fingers, jaw issues, brain matters… It was just along a stretch of a highway. We saw people sitting on porches looking kind of weird. We said nothing to each other until later.

ALCOHOL FREE AREAS

I went out looking for beer one day. I was living in a beer free County (There were also Hard Liquor free counties as well). I asked a neighbor where/how to buy it as there was none in the stores. They pointed down the road and told me where to turn off to get some at an illegal stand.

They explained there was a drive-through and you could just go down the driveway, pay out back, drive forward and you would get your beer and then leave.

I went on down the road and found the turnoff. Realized a County Sheriff had gone down the road just ahead of me! There was no way to get out of there so I figured I was screwed and just might as well stay.

The Sheriff stopped in front of me and I waited. The deputy laughed at whatever the clerk said, and took something from them, laughed again and took off to the pickup place. So, I figured they probably had to shut down.

But I pulled ahead anyway, ordered, and paid and pulled ahead to pick up my case. Was a great place to do business and I told everyone I knew.

So, everything worked out fine. Apparently being a dry County didn't mean as much as one might think. You just couldn't buy it at normal outlets!

MORE JOBMOBILE WORK

My final few months strictly involved working the Jobmobile Program. I would plan my week out, where I would be what I would do, etc. Lots of on the road time to make it around to everywhere.

JOBMOBILE VAN

I finally got my Vista Jobmobile Van via the local Social Services Agency.

Went to a local business that could help me get them modified and mounted. I had the signs adorned with the word JOB MOBILE as well as the names of the supporting local agencies..

Then I had it mounted on the passenger side of the van. Thereafter, I began my Jobmobile duties- with an official looking vehicle that could be seen from a distance.

MY FIRST JOBMOBILE CONTACT/VISIT

I recall the first little community I went into where I started interviewing people regarding JOBMOBILE. Very first person was a nice older woman. I explained what I was doing, and she burst into tears, which shocked me.

Her husband had died a month or so earlier and she continued to come to grips with it. She said it was very painful because none of her friends were coming by. She teared constantly and it was painful for both of us. After about five minutes I went to another house down the road.

While working the Jobmobile Program, I went to a chicken farm to ask about their hiring. He was pretty desperate and tried to hire me! I said no but I did buy two dozen eggs before I left! He said he would take anyone willing to work, regardless of race.

So many businesses, especially farmers, wanting to hire right away. Farming of course was a business that had high labor for only about 6 to 8 months.

But this was at a time when younger people, especially Blacks, were moving North. There was factory work in the North and Northeast and that drew a lot of kids there. Thus, the labor shortage in some areas.

And my DRUNKEN DRIVING!

One night while driving fairly drunk on the way back from an all Vista party by myself I found myself driving behind a car with a couple of other vistas. We were all going to the same residence to spend the night. They were driving a little slow. I was in a drunken playful mood. They had to stop at a stop sign.

I suddenly decided to cut across an open field. That turned out to be somebody's freshly sodded front yard!

I drove halfway across it when my overworked vehicle began to slow down. BUT I just kept going, slower and slower. Someone on a porch was looking at me!

I finally made it back up onto the highway ahead of my friends and beat them home. After that, everyone seemed afraid of me for a while. I avoided that stretch of road for several days AND got the mud off my tires.

TRANSYLVANIANS

Nearby was a City called Bat Cave. It was named after an actual BAT CAVE! We explored the area and there definitely was a large cavern in the side of the mountain that went in a long way. Lots of bats did fly in and out depending on the time of day (and number of tourists)!

We went into the City of Bat Cave to see who/what was there. We went door to door meeting people. People that live there often had stories about scary things that had occurred.

Turns out that they were descendants of people from Europe. The County was called Transylvania County and numerous of the people originated from the actual Country of Transylvania.

We heard stories of scary creatures that came out at night. The tales likely came from lore passed down over the generations.

One woman told us about a creature that would sometimes fly into someone's home where there was a newborn infant. Allegedly they would land on the child and drink the mother's milk off the infant's lips or out of its mouth and, in the process, kill it! We didn't explore that any further, (though later I thought it might have been SIDs).

OTHER SCARY THINGS

Gail and her sister who was visiting her, were followed for a few miles. they stopped and visited a friend, when they came back out, 3 guys ask them "what do you think of the people here?"

This had begun a week earlier but, nothing had happened since. In a few weeks, tourists would be swamping through, so the locals would have other concerns.

BURT LANCASTER

We stopped in a small town called Lancaster. While driving around we stopped to talk to a guy working in his garden. He was the Minister of the local Church. He explained how tough it was to get known in such a town.

He said he was known as a newcomer because he had **only** lived there for 25 years. He said he and his children were somewhat accepted but not entirely. They partook in the more public local activities but not in the familial, personal events.

We went to his next Sunday service. It was very much like a Stereotypical Black service. After they all got comfortable with us, various members confessed sins, cried out, prayed their souls out.

We left the day of the Church service. Before we left the area, I insisted we drive around until we found a mailbox with the name BURT Lancaster on it and eventually, we did! Nice old residence that fit in with all the others, but I finally saw his home!?

VISTA from ANOTHER GROUP

One VISTA (Did not come in with our group) was quite a nuisance (to the other VISTAs). He worked mainly by himself. He made lots of Black friends which was cool, but I was told he lorded it over the rest of the VISTAs in his area.

The first and only time I met him he was in a hospital. My VISTA friends asked me to accompany them because they thought he was quite an a**hole and they wanted someone else to come along.

At the hospital he was in a bed in a convalescent ward. He was being visited by several Blacks from the community. As he talked to us, I understood why they did not like him. The Black men just wandered aimlessly around the room while he ranted and lectured us about what we were not doing.

He finally said that he had fallen off his porch and had broken his back. He was going to be in a wheelchair the rest of his life. We left shortly thereafter with a mixture of pity and anger. He just drove my friends (and eventually would have me) crazy.

RETURNING THE JOBMOBILE VAN

I had to return my van to the General Services Administration along the Coast. It had a lot of usage and I had to have the sign removed before I headed over. But the hole sites were still there, and I had also done some damage.

I was nervous about bringing it back. And as I was driving along, a brick fell off a truck and knocked out my mirror on the way! BUT I just kept going.

I finally got to the garage where I drop it off. I waited there while a guy came up. I had all my excuses and explanations ready to go about all the damage.

He then just came over to me and said he had the flu and could hardly see or stand. So, I quickly grabbed the replacement car keys I needed and drove out of there before he had a good look. Again, as so many times before during the year, I got away clean.

The CHASE

When driving from the coast back to our VISTA residence, I came up upon a car with four White guys and it is chasing a car with four Black guys. The white guys were honking swerving the Blacks. I am guessing they were trying to intimidate them.

Finally, as the car with the four Blacks came to an exit and left the freeway (the exit I was taking), the Whites car kept going. But at the last moment the car with the Blacks suddenly swerved, crossed the exit barrier, and got back onto the highway. They were the ones doing the chasing and screaming. The last I saw the Whites were looking back while the Blacks were laughing and yelling as they honked continuously. I have no clue as to what

RIOTS

One of our VISTAs came home one night all panicky. He said there was a riot warming up in our local downtown. Police and Whites on one side, Blacks alone on the other. He said it never fully turned into a riot, but it was becoming a stressful face off. He said he couldn't take it anymore, so he just got out of there.

We saw nothing about it in the news the next day or days. It's like nothing ever happened. That lack of coverage was common regarding race interactions in those days.

ANGELA DAVIS

One night we got word that Angela Davis was being brought through our town. They were taking her to Florida, and they were trying to throw off the police. She allegedly would be coming through from California being transferred from and to various cars.

We never heard anything about it, but we were stressed a couple days. Nothing ever made the newspaper, but it was panicky for us. Did NOT want to see her killed or captured!

COIN TOSSING

I was traveling with another Vista and he showed me where a train came through the area near the Public Swimming Pool. The train dutifully slowed down, and the engineer leaned way out of the cab and tossed a handful of coins to the mostly Black children. They would all stop swimming or playing and run for the coins.

My friend thought it was demeaning while I thought it was so cool! When I was a kid, I would have taken spare change from ANYONE (or so I have been told).

BEGINNING OF THE END
MOON LANDING

The July 1969 moon launch was quite the event. We had a TV, but it was a mess. A local Social Worker invited us to his house. We all, except Mike, went to watch the launching.

His TV was Color! The roof antenna rotated until it got the best signal. He provided us with beer and cokes and CHIPS and other snacks. We were like kings and queens!

We watched intently as they approached the moon. We saw them land. Eventually we watched them step off the ship and onto the ground. It was beautiful to see as the color TV was so clear.

Suddenly, the picture went to hell. There was some mess caused by the camera facing the sun and cooking its insides. The backup camera made our TV viewing like we would have had back at our place with our real cheap

TV. However, it was the best you could have gotten eventually.

But it was an eventful and unforgettable time for us and the rest of the World!

To make it even more interesting we later heard from one of our members. He had gone down to Florida with a couple who wanted to watch the launch with some of their NASA friends at the site.

He agreed with us re the Landing being wonderful. He also noted he had seen the Lift-Off in person! He was with his friends and NUMEROUS NASA staffers. He said it was wonderful, exciting, and unforgettable.

BUT he said later that night things changed. He said they went back to the motel room they shared. But others began to show up. Finally, the room was filled with other young couples.

That night, he explained, what the couple he went down there with did was to WIFE SWAP with other NASA STAFFERS!

We asked if HE joined in. He again explained he was engaged but ALSO you had to have a spouse/mate there as well. Apparently, those are the rules and they apparently worked. You needed a partner if you wanted to join in. Go figure.

(I shortly after VISTA got a Government job and there was a TON of ON THE JOB relationships that avoided telling one's spouses, but that is another story for another day)

He said he sat in the motel room while people would come in and pick up a room key that would take them to a room for another swap!

So, he just sat there as people came and went, making small talk - the best he could do under these most ridiculous circumstances he found himself in.

He said the couple he had gone down there with confessed they had swapped even in their little city. They were teachers at the local College, and apparently it was what people did in those days, even in the South.

(A couple years later when I was working for a rural Federal Agency, one of the employees said they wife swapped the previous winter. He said it was deadly cold and snowy and so it began. He said about 10 couples, including he and his wife joined in the festivities.

He explained he was the only one who didn't remarry as his wife left him for someone else!)

GOODBYES

The moon landing was just about our final event as a team/group. We did a couple more things, but nothing was as eventful as sharing the Moon Landing.

We had a couple drinking parties, threw our darts together one last time, swam in our Lake and then it was time.

IN A FEW DAYS, WE SAID OUR GOODBYES AT THE AIRPORT. I WAS THE FIRST OF OUR GROUP TO DEPART. I WAVED TO MY FRIENDS ONE LAST TIME AS MY PLANE ROLLED DOWN THE RUNWAY.

OTHERS BEGAN LEAVING A COUPLE WEEKS LATER. WE DID NOT SEE EACH OTHER AGAIN FOR NEARLY TWENTY YEARS!

PART VI

My EXPERIENCE IN JOBMOBILE:

THE ACTUAL REPORT

As promised above, the below is my OFFICIAL and UNEDITED report on JOBMOBILE, written in July of 1969 and turned over to the Henderson County Social Services Office. The report itself is word for word what I submitted except for the names of individuals.

NOTE: As a VISTA Volunteer in 1969 located in a rural County in North Carolina I was assigned the task of testing the feasibility of starting a Mobile Jobs Program. This involved my using a van to travel around the County back roads setting up shop at stores or wherever people might gather. My role was to work with Social Service Agencies and the Employment offices trying to match potential employees with actual jobs.

Following is the REPORT I wrote summarizing my efforts which I turned into the local Social Services Agency. It contains the basic stats and kinds and types of efforts made as well as successes and failures. Nothing has been edited or modified except for the removal of identifying information like addresses, last names, and birth dates.

REPORT SUBMITTED IN AUGUST OF 1969

The purpose of Jobmobile was to reach and find employment for the rural disadvantaged of Henderson County, NC. Employment was not the only concern. Information from the various community agencies was to be made available. This included the Department of Social Services (DSS,) the Employment Security Commission (ESC) and Components of Western Carolina Community Action (WCCA). Their total parts were: The Sheltered Workshop, guidance counseling, Head start, the Neighborhood Youth Corps and other programs encountering the poor.

My part was to choose routes and stopping points, schedule times and drive the interviewer and the Representative from Welfare to the various points. Also, I was to follow up on the people we contacted and help them attain the job that employment security sent them out to. This meant the keeping of records on each person, helping to get them in for their interview, if necessary, and contacting them for a period of up to six months.

ACTUAL RUNNING

Originally scheduled as stops were:

1) Mon, 9-11 am Hooper's Creek;

2) Mon, 1-3 Bishops Store, Dana;

3) Wed, 9-11 Ed Griffiths Store, Edneyville.

4) Wed, 1-3 Crab Creek Store, Crab Creek.

The places were chosen by ESC (EMPLOYMENT SECURITY DIVISION) and the Department of Social Services.

They based their choices on their records of the number of unemployed and the number on Welfare.

The first stop, Hooper's Creek Grocery, located in Hooper's Creek, did not need such a service. The owner of the Store, Mrs. R. knows everyone in the local community.

In her opinion, there was no one who was looking for work who did not now have it. However, the extent to which people there are underemployed is hard to judge.

Something along these lines should be investigated. There are, as elsewhere in Henderson County, a great number of elderly people on welfare and unemployed. This area has a need for training programs to teach job skills.

There is a sense of community here that I did not find in too many other areas. There are few hardcore unemployed.

Bishop's Store, in Dana, is quite rural and lacking in contact with Social Service Agencies. More people responded to JobMobile in Dana than in Hooper's Creek. They were mostly young but were some hard core unemployed. Overall, there was not as much of a feeling of community as in Hooper's creek. Bishops store is a very central location for that area. Dana can use the full Jobmobile Service, especially guidance counseling.

Ed G.'s store in Edneyville is one of many along US 64. There are small stores scattered about. It is impossible to catch everyone at one store at a fixed time. The Edneyville area is huge and cannot possibly be covered by one stop.

The poor are most often elderly, but still the full services of Jobmobile would be practical. What is need is a better system.

Crab Creek Store on Kanuga Drive is still a mystery. There are two communities: Nearby Crab Creek and Holly Springs. Holly springs is very much in need of the full services. I don't believe it has much contact with Hendersonville in any way. Crab Creek is not as isolated.

Mr. L. can give some info on each of these areas.

There are quite a few elderlies in Holly Springs. Some I would consider to be hard core poverty. There is much that could be done there. There are a few people that can be contacted to get a fuller picture listed below.

Jobmobile was not at all successful contacting people there. Few people showed interest. I never got to know any one person or get a feel for the area. As far as can be assessed, there I see a need for Jobmobile. However, it will never come off without contact by a community worker.

In the short time that I was at Red A.'s store in Bat Cave, I contacted about seven people. According to the Community Worker there is a need for Jobmobile. That is also my opinion. The area is not united or able to be called a community.

The Brickton Church Annex is the only all Black area Jobmobile contacted. It is a well-defined community. All services are needed here. There is high unemployment. As in Dana, motivational counseling is necessary. The people are responsive to what JOBMOBILE has to offer, even though few seemed to understand what was going on.

Brickton is an example of how a Community worker can help make such a program workable. A lot of my acceptance was due to their work.

In general, all store owners were cooperative. They had no qualms about what we wanted to do. Most were skeptical about the number of unemployed but were willing to do everything they could to help out.

Publicity included radio WHKP, bulletin boards and two news articles. This was supplemented by posters at each store, handbills printed up, and signs used on the van. After this,

Publicity was created through word of mouth by community workers, but only to a limited degree.

The van itself was underequipped with just a table and three chairs in the back. Those trying had great difficulty getting into the truck. There was no filing system beyond a small metal Box xxx with the ESC job forms, alphabetized.

It was most limited in that there was no list of Jobs in the JOBMOBILE for immediate placement. I believe the truck was under equipped for this experiment.

There was a wide variety of people met and signed up. The majority were under 18. The next largest groups were from 18-21. Then over 21. A great number of people stopped to talk. Most people felt that "anyone who wants work can find it." Or "ESC can't find you no jobs." And "I haven't heard a word out of them for nearly a year."

They all seemed willing to talk about their areas. Two questions I found valuable were: "<u>What do you do for kicks around here?</u>" and "<u>What do most people do around here?</u>" These questions open just about anyone who is at ease with me. I met no hostility or resentment from anyone or any community.

In Hooper's Creek, Mrs. R. at the Hooper's Creek Store, can give a very complete picture of her area. She is the center of the community for practical information. She knows what everyone is doing or not doing. This is true to some degree with all the store owners.

Since most everyone shops at their store in their immediate area, storekeepers have a pretty accurate picture of their area. As an introduction it would be important to talk with the storekeepers. BUT I think it is a myth to believe that they are good spreaders of the word. Some do some of the time, others never.

The follow-up portion of the program was quite difficult. I know what happened to most of those who showed up without having to make contacts.

Few who got signed up ever got work. This included some whom I thought were professionally qualified. Some got work on their own. So, follow up activities by me became ridiculous. We had nothing to say when they asked when they would get work.

JOBMOBILE traveled, from Hendersonville some 540 miles in the three months it ran. Side-work, follow-up and contacts were another 600 miles. It was at stores approximately 64 hours. There were never more than four stops per week on more than two days.

After the first four weeks, JOBMOBILE quit running for two hours at each place and was cut to one. Also, the times of day were changed from mornings and afternoons to late afternoons and evenings. This change was made by talking to community workers and residents of each area. It seems that no matter how poor a person is he can always find some odd job to do during the morning or afternoon. Therefore, it makes more sense to try the evenings.

As a result of JOBMOBILE, five people found work out of 26 who officially signed up. I met personally better than 40 other people.

When a company hires an illiterate or dropout the company soon loses him. Industries must strive to set up introductory programs designed to hold onto their workers. I have heard of too many companies willing to let people go rather than work out their problems

Notable exceptions appear to be JP Stevens and Gerber. An association of businesses such as the one John L. (Social Worker) was working on would be of great benefit to workers. It would not change the industries procedures too much, but it would enable a worker to function in a plan.

In job development, help is needed for women. Few jobs and few training programs are available for women. From what I hear, there are enough jobs for trained women. Also, a greater variety of jobs are needed. There are too few jobs outside of factory work for women

In the future JOBMOBILE should not be run on a scheduled basis as it was by myself. It should be run based on need. Vistas and community workers should be made aware of JOBMOBILE and be on the lookout for persons they feel might benefit. If jobs are a problem or are brought up as such at a meeting, then the JOBMOBILE rep should go out and meet with them. Then whatever system that meets the problem could be set up for that area.

Under no circumstances should JOBMOBILE be set up again without contacts in each area. JOBMOBILE should not be artificially enforced onto and area, but should to some degree, be wanted.

This should be done by designing it to offer a broad variety of programs.

JOBMOBILE could be most efficiently run by two people. One involved in contacting the people using the services while the other works with the technical support, businesses, and the various agencies. It is simply too much work for one person. It can bring a person to a complete standstill just trying to work on publicity. Two would be more likely to come up with fresh new ideas.

Publicity for whatever is set up should be primarily through word of mouth. In keeping with my idea not to run JOBMOBILE as before, if the desire for JOBMOBILE or jobs comes out of a community, publicity would be simple. It would then be a matter of reminding people. In covering scattered areas, I do have a few suggestions.

Someone should talk to storeowners, gas station attendants and anyone else who encounters local people. If they are informed, they can at least answer questions anyone might have.

BUT I would not depend solely on them for publicity on the local level.

Community workers should also explain the process to Minsters and organized clubs. Again, the minister or club member should not simply be given a piece of paper to read but should have an understanding of what the program involves. The newspapers should have notices in the Help Wanted Section. I found the papers and radio less effective than word of mouth but there were some incidences when people did respond to the media.

RECOMMMENDATIONS

It cannot be over-emphasized how important the VISTAs and community workers are to this type of program. JOBMOBILE should be open to the idea of making contacts at any time suggested by the outreach people.

In attempting to bring businesses into an area, it is important to get a definite list of people who would be available to work. This has been done by the City of Clinton, NC. The results of their efforts can be obtained by writing the Clinton Chamber of Commerce.

In the Asheville area, there is a quota set by industries as to how large a labor force they want in that area.

Besides legal action, a guaranteed labor force would enable an industry to come in when not wanted by other companies.

One good method for exchanging information would be a community bulletin board. People could put messages on it, help wanted notices, those available for work, rides offered, etc. I have found that communication is a problem here as elsewhere.

Word does not get around as easily as many people think. The word is beaten, kicked, and mutilated beyond recognition by the time it gets "around." A system of exchange such as a bulletin board might be a step toward enabling the word to make its appointed rounds without essential damage to its original meaning. This bulletin board could be in a small structure built specifically for that, a store, garage, church, or anywhere else people congregate.

In getting the ALL-IMPORTANT JOB LIST, it is important that businesses be contacted personally. A rapport must be established between JOBMOBILE and businesses.

EMPLOYMENT SECURITY COMMISSION

Contrary to expectations, ESC did not fully cooperate with us. They were not aggressive in finding jobs. Word seemed to get around in the areas that ESC could not find jobs. They did not send interviewers out with the JOBMOBILE.

It was as if JOBMOBILE had to prove itself before getting cooperation. This was a hindrance in making it a legitimate program and was awfully hard on me. No one person should be left to carry out a program of this nature.

Mr. I. of ESSC was enthusiastic about JOBMOBILE but appeared to be holding back his opinions and suggestions. The feeling I was left with was that the ESC was simply not determined enough to find the jobs.

DEPARTMENT OF SOCIAL SERVICES

It is not exactly clear in my mind now what their role was to be. Mr. I. and I never did discuss JOBMOBILE until the close of the program. He would be quite helpful and cooperative in any program one might come up with. Again, he wasn't willing to take aggressive advantage of the outreach potential

WCCA

Jack G. gave JOBMOBILE the initial boost to get it going. I wish now that he would have shown more interest or made it more apparent to me. Also, it would have helped to have him work with me on pinpointing more of the problems I was having With ESC and DSS.

HELPFUL PEOPLE

Mrs. R. Hooper Creek. Friendly, informative, helpful for general and specific information.

Rev A. Lives in Skyland- ask at Crab Creek Grocery for directions. Knows all about Crab Creek Community.

Rev C. Also ask about at the store above. Knows of Holly Springs Community.

Mr. L. Knows about Holly Springs.

Red of Andersons Grocery, Bat Cave… Quite cooperative will help in any way he can.

Donny, his father, owns 5 points (formerly Bishops) store in Dana. He talked about the class differences between people from Hendersonville vs Rural areas.

There was a big enough difference to keep him from going to various places of amusement as often as he wanted. (He and other rural folk were called Hillbillies).

Coke Delivery man. Complained about lack of job security. He was worried about having an accident and losing his present position. This would cut his pay. He also knew of people from OLIN fired too easily

Resident of Dana Complained about GE, Low pay, and difficulty of work requirements.

Resident of Brickton. Many on third shift (night where new workers go)

racist. Believes he himself quit because of it.

Personnel Manager, probably unaware of this problem. He wonders why Brickton does not have more people working at Cranston. If racism does not exist, this info should be made available.

Mrs. C. On Kanuga Drive. Supposed to know about Crab Creek Community. About 3 miles out of Henderson just before the lake. B. her husband

E. of Jeter Mt. Lives in Crab Creek. Poor, needs work, could be a good contact.

PEOPLE CONTACTED AND SIGNED UP

D., S.

S., O-

D., F.

L., H.,

J., H.,

B., C.,

D., V.

D., E,

F., M.,

G., P.

K., G.

H., D.

H., M.

H., W.,

J., D. J.,

K., R.,

L., R,

M., C.,

M., J. H,

P., J.,

R., D. A.,

S., C. R.,

S., C.M.

T., J.

S. S.,

P, T,

BUSINESS CONTACTS

DUPONT

Personnel supervisor

Plant manager: Family man with dependents, mostly hard-core cases

CRANSTON PRINT WORKS

Mgr.

Quite interested in doing what he can.

Quite cooperative.

GE

General Manager

GERBER BABY FOOD

E. plant manager

Quite cooperative

TAYLOR INSTRUMENTS

Ardon, NC 28704

M., industrial relations Manager.

BERKLY

Mgr.,

PART VII

ENDING

As noted, before, the above was my official report. All names and addresses were changed or abbreviated from the official Report.

On the back cover is a newspaper article about what Jobmobile was all about. As noted above, they did have me deconstruct the VAN just before I left so I imagine it was not picked up BUT maybe the above report was what they needed to make decisions.

To me, Jobmobile was a great way to reach people outside the normal modes. Most unemployed or underemployed I met, wanted something better and hopefully they got it.

MISCELLANY

So that/this was VISTA for me. One year of ever-growing interest. No days, except a few, were ever boring.

After a while you got over the point you were an outsider living in someone else's State.

When I got to North Carolina - especially for the first couple of weeks, when I slept, I would dream like I was still back in Portland. Same old, events, issues. It took at least people two weeks for my mind to switch over to the new situation. The same was true in reverse.

I came home for a couple weeks in January and it took most of my time to switch back to Portland. BUT when I went back to NC, I immediately was "back."

When I returned to Portland the following Summer, it took nearly two weeks to get "back".

Even watching the weather on TV in Portland, it took a while to adjust from one State to the other. When I got back to Oregon, I kept looking to see what was occurring in North Carolina like that might mean something.

In August of 1969, I flew out of a small airport to Charlotte then to O'Hare and finally to Portland, Oregon. Family and friends were as happy to see me as I was to see them!

MET SO MANY GOOD PEOPLE AND HAD SO MANY WONDERFUL EVENTS THAT YEAR. IT HAS BEEN VIRTUALLY IMPOSSIBLE TO FORGET (that which I can still remember!).

THE END

Made in the USA
Middletown, DE
01 September 2020

17063190R00125